WHAT WAS LOST

What Was Lost

Seeking Refuge
in the Psalms

a spiritual memoir

—❧—

Maureen O'Brien

To Mad,
you are the best
daughter ever.
love
Mom
4/21

franciscan
media®
Cincinnati, Ohio

LIBRARY OF CONGRESS CATALOGING-IN-PUBLICATION DATA
Names: O'Brien, Maureen, 1960- author.
Title: What was lost : seeking refuge in the Psalms : a spiritual memoir / Maureen O'Brien.
Description: Cincinnati, Ohio : Franciscan Media, [2021] | Includes bibliographical references. | Summary: "By praying and living with the Psalms through the trials and joys of life, Maureen O'Brien discovered healing, refuge, and a deep faith in God. Here she shares those discoveries with readers who are on their own journeys of faith"– Provided by publisher.
Identifiers: LCCN 2020044894 (print) | LCCN 2020044895 (ebook) | ISBN 9781632533432 | ISBN 9781632533449 (ebook)
Subjects: LCSH: Bible. Psalms–Meditations. | O'Brien, Maureen, 1960- | Catholic women–Religious life.
Classification: LCC BS1430.54 .O27 2021 (print) | LCC BS1430.54 (ebook) | DDC 282.092 [B]–dc23
LC record available at https://lccn.loc.gov/2020044894
LC ebook record available at https://lccn.loc.gov/2020044895

Cover and book design by Mark Sullivan
Copyright ©2021, Maureen O'Brien. All rights reserved.
ISBN 978-1-63253-343-2

Published by Franciscan Media
28 W. Liberty St.
Cincinnati, OH 45202
www.FranciscanMedia.org

Printed in the United States of America.
Printed on acid-free paper.
21 22 23 24 25   5 4 3 2 1

Seek /sēk/ verb
gerund or present participle: seeking
To attempt to find (something):
"they came here to seek shelter
from biting winter winds"

Contents

Introduction: What Was Lost

I never went looking for the psalms. They went looking for *me*. I was simply a broken woman, spiritually and physically. In the bare space where my husband's dresser once stood, I had placed a lamp and a rug remnant, and I thumbtacked a jewel-toned postcard of a Blessed Mother painting by Lippi. I set an intention that each dawn I'd sit cross-legged on the floor and read 1 Corinthians 13:4, the timeless passage about love. I lit a candle and prayed the sort of prayer that crosses over into begging: *Please*.

As a writer, I believe in the power of words, in their necessity and beauty. One of the main aspects of Catholicism that has kept me coming back is the lushness, the intensity, and the fervor of how language is used within the faith. Not just in the liturgy of a daily or Sunday Mass, but especially in the sacraments. There are few words that have ever meant as much to me as the wedding vows I spoke; for over twenty-three years as a wife and mother, I built a life upon those promises to stay true in good times and bad, in sickness and in health. And then, suddenly (though it was not sudden), my husband no longer lived in our home. I believed if I prayed as hard as I could, I could pray our marriage into finding a new beginning. That my life with my husband and children would be restored. And so I underlined the passage and read it over and over, how love is patient and kind. How love never fails. I figured that if I went back to all the words spoken at our ceremony, I could find the golden thread and begin the repair. It seemed to me that since Jesus was with us on that altar when these words were read, when we became husband and wife, then he was with us still and would do everything to help us mend the ever-widening tatters.

I was tattered. My body was still recovering from the losses brought by two years of cancer surgeries. I suppose the phrase is *my ass was kicked*. Because as I sat there, I was recovering also from a freak accident that summer of falling in my own driveway and shattering my left wrist so badly that it was gone. And by gone, I mean the bones were now dust, and not returning, replaced with a plate and many screws. I had permanently lost the hand I knew. My X-fix, the first of many devices in a long year of trying to put me back together, had two tall screws that were whirled into me, one along the bones near my thumb, the other stuck up along a bloody incision higher up my arm. Poetically (in the words of my surgeon) this was to help connect the places that were broken to the places that were whole. An eight-inch black metal rod connected the screws. It was grotesque. Yellow push pins stuck out along my thumb and in my wrist underneath. Eventually this was surgically removed and I had to spend three hours a day in other plastic devices, just sitting.

I guess I have always been a fighter, and I credit my father for that. Perhaps there is something to the legacy of being the daughter of a scrappy Irishman, because I hunched there, in my bedroom, in the most pain I had ever felt, shocked that my shattered wrist was immeasurably more excruciating than cancer had been, and I begged hard. I was determined, in those hours I was not at work, in having to strap myself into those strange devices, that I would pray.

One thing I can tell you is that a paperback from college can save your life. A worthless—money-wise—book with a spine of glue so old it's hard and cracked can become a precious pearl. And this is what happened to me. I began by seeking out the famous quote of love and in my one-handed clumsiness my Bible fell, and it too broke, and permanently opened right to Book 1 of the Psalms. Psalm 23, to be exact. I decided to read it out loud and could hardly see the verses through my tears as my voice wavered. *He makes me lie down in green pastures.* How exhausted I was, how alone and in need of care, suffering each night with pain-induced insomnia. *Even though I walk through a valley dark as death.* I was terrified of my cancer returning. *Dwell in the house of the Lord.* I could no longer afford our home, so where would I go? Did I already have a place of shelter with God?

When the closing sentence used the words *love unfailing*, something shifted in me. I'd never considered *God's* love as abiding. Lasting. Unshakeable. Though I was still unable to admit that my marriage was lost, my eyes were drawn to this new pairing of words. My concentration skills were weak. I began reading through the pages in wild, random order. Psalm 140, then 91, back to 6, skipping to 144, thumbing backward and forward, from the bottom of the pages to the top. *Love unfailing* kept popping out, sometimes reversed as *unfailing love.* I was in over my head, in the pain of my own life, and I knew it. My once-solid world was now—to use psalm imagery—swept away in a flood. But there was something about these poems penned over 2,500 years ago, confidently trusting in the embankment of this enduring love, that kept me from going under.

How had I not ever found their artistry before? In my lifetime of sitting at Mass, I'd listened to sopranos sing them from the lectern, and then lift up their open palms inviting me to join in on the response. I had almost always stayed silent. I began to think about all the women who sang the psalms to me. I pictured their pantsuits, the pastel beads of their necklaces, hair fixed up nicely, swept back from their faces. How earnestly they worked to enunciate all the words so we would hear them fully and clearly: *deer, water, broken, rescue me*. I thought of the way they waited for their cues by gazing back at the choir loft. When at last I discovered the psalms, it was those gifted cantors who first led me on that path with their soulful, motherly voices filling the rafters with sustained notes. They'd shown me those words are meant to be sung.

So as the autumn unfolded and I had to sit in those devices, and then divorce drew near, and then having to find another home drew near, I made a new promise to read one psalm aloud as the very first thing I did each morning. I did not check my email, read the newspaper, or speak on the phone until I'd spent time in contemplation. Instead of just reading them in my head, I found that my emotions flowed when I spoke the words, and ensured I did not rush. In essence, speaking them all alone in my bedroom was a form of simple singing. I had no lute, or harp, or lyre; I was without a pipe organ or a baby grand piano. I had only my wavering voice accompanied by the rustle of the tissue-thin pages.

I will respectfully leave the close analysis of the structures of these poems to the scholars who can really dig in, but what startled me over and over in so many of the psalms is the emotional contrast. First there's often a lament, not sugar-coated or minimized, not swept away or judged. Instead, the suffering is eloquently described. For example, the early lines of Psalm 69: "I am wearied with crying out, my throat is sore." Guilt, shame, reproach, and bitterness follow. Then, a *but* appears. "But I lift up this prayer to thee." Over and over I found these sudden reversals.

How did they make sense? After a few months of this daily morning practice, I understood the pattern. I would read many lines of anguish.

Once the painful truths are expressed, in detail, not rushed, there's a sense of being deeply heard and listened to—heard by God. Once that internal, intimate ache is honored, we find space in our heavy hearts to move around. We can take that leap of faith and trust, again and again. What the psalms began to teach me is to stay true to my human grief, to articulate it, to bring the fear and frustration straight to God. By doing that, faith will appear, often suddenly, always the balm we have been seeking.

Because I was going through such a raw time, I often found passages about disgrace. I will simply say that I was thunderstruck by the events that unfurled. Sometimes I underlined words that might have once seemed archaic but now rang true. *Enemies, lowly, ambush, abyss.* Yes, I was ashamed. On the page with Psalm 25 my deep blue ink jumps out *shame, shame, shame.* Other more hopeful words impacted me. In particular, *refuge* became the most medicinal word of all. When I return to that paperback now, it breaks my heart to see all the "refuges" I underlined.

There is refuge throughout, over and over.

And there are many broken bones, longing to heal.

I learned how to live with 50 percent of my wrist gone. I learned to reach for change, always, with my right hand. I had to accept a new identity as a divorced Catholic. There were factors so far beyond my control. As another year went by, I continued with the practice of starting my day with a psalm. In Psalm 56 I read, "I have bound myself with vows to thee." Was it possible to focus on a *new* vow? I believed it was.

I was alone, but I was alive.

> For my soul has been freed from death, my eyes from tears, my feet from stumbling,
> I shall walk before the Lord in the land of the living." (Ps 116: 8-9)

As the darkness in my life receded, I began to see the lighter aspects of the psalms. Like the opening of Psalm 116, "I love the Lord… who turned an ear to me the day I called" (1-2). There is so much joy, praise, and celebration. Admittedly, it has been a long road. When I was first separated, a very good friend of mine who is a therapist said, "It can take five years to heal from this." I thought, "Oh, no, that's not going to be me."

But it has taken that long. I have been given much grace, including the stamina to continue with this spiritual practice these last seven years. I still have a place on the floor of my bedroom—a different bedroom in a different house—and my still-falling-apart-Bible. I just can't give that paperback up; it has been with me so many years, and if I had to choose a favorite sound, it would still be the whisper of the tissue-thin pages.

As for the soprano who lifts her hand in the Responsorial Psalm and invites me in? Yesterday at Mass, after having been contemplating all this, I decided I should thank her. She does such a stunning job for our very lively inner-city Franciscan church. She clutched her music binder and I was headed toward her, but she stepped toward an elderly man by the altar hunched crookedly in his wheelchair. She greeted him warmly and kissed him on the cheek. He lifted his head, eyes shining, and opened his mouth, ready to sing.

Seeking the Psalms

Tree Pietas

It isn't just the water that calms me down and helps me let go of my anxieties when I'm walking. It's also the thousands of pines, oaks, and maples stretching wide, growing higher into the sky. There is a phenomenon—if there's a scientific name, I don't know of it—where the trees break and fall into one another's arms. I've come to call these *tree pietas*. A ripped branch catches at an angle in the V-shape of a nearby tree, and the stronger tree holds it. Almost always, each walk brings me to the angular shapes of a newly formed, geometric tree pieta. Often, an entire tree weakens, no longer able to stand upright, and instead of falling horizontally on the ground, its trunk is being cradled within the branches of the taller, vigorous tree.

I'm now a seeker of these tree pietas, because they remind me of how the psalms catch me. Something tender stirs within me when I see the connections of these trees. When I myself need to let go of parts of my life, or my spirits are falling, the lines and stanzas of the psalms catch me and keep me there. Sometimes my need for support is as random as flipping open to a page and finding "He blows with his wind and the waters flow." Where I was once breaking and falling, I am now embraced by the words and held aloft in their branches.

The Highway at Night

I feel vulnerable in admitting how many miles I've driven alone in the last six or seven years since my divorce and my new life as an empty nester. I'm not sure why it brings up feelings of shame, because one of the reasons I've spent so much time on the highway at night is a wonderful one; I've been driving home from visiting my daughter who lives outside Boston. Though I've been alone at the steering wheel navigating between the headlights of the eighteen-wheelers, I often have late night jazz on for company. There's nothing like the beauty of familiar melodies, a saxophone filling my car as I see I am still an hour from home.

The streetlights, the overhead beams especially bright along the exits, suggest a metaphor to me. I glide into the edge of the circle of light, enter the whitest, pearliest part as it illuminates my hands on the steering wheel, then drive out of it, with only my headlights slicing through the night. Again I am in shadow, with darkness all around me.

This metaphor of flickering in light and dark as I try to return home is why I turn to the psalms. The contrasts of life, especially when I am tired (and I am often tired) overwhelm me. Not just my own suffering and healing, but the sorrows and joys of those I love so much. The "I" in the psalms pours out with exposed honesty, a human struggling to find God within the world. This voice speaks for me. Not because I can't speak for myself, but because sometimes my emotional vocabulary is limited. The "I" is a phenomenal poet articulating deep despair and sweeping faith, giving me all the words I need to keep driving, switching lanes through the night.

Tiny Purses

When I was a very little girl attending Mass every Sunday with my father and older sister, the dress code was very different than it is today. Admittedly, I find relief in the casual atmosphere now permitted at

Mass. I'm loath to wear jeans and sneakers only because I was raised "old school," but I do see that now people feel welcomed no matter their attire, and I feel that's the way church should be.

Still, I love recalling the Easter mantillas I wore. Circles of patterned white lace, each one came with scalloped edges and a comb woven in so we could keep it snugly in place on top of our heads. Besides the mantillas, dresses with velvet sashes, and white tights, we also wore white gloves and, to add to the accessories, carried purses. We had nothing to put in the purses, of course, except thin handkerchiefs dotted with violets, too fancy to ever actually use. I proudly held the handle of that purse, and, bored during Mass, I recall playing with the brass clasp, turning it to open it, peering in, then clicking it shut.

The memory of those vinyl purses I clutched when I was very small comes to me now as I age. The metaphor of the emptiness I carry still, in my heart, along with the expectation—no, not expectation, but hope—it's hope in doing the next right thing. "I cry aloud to God.... My hands are stretched out unceasingly" (Ps 77:2–3). Like undoing the clasp, opening the purse, and knowing something essential will come if you just believe the dark inner corners will be filled.

Crosses on the Highway

I've never forgotten the beauty of the bold white crosses on the highway.

One of the most life-altering displays of faith I've ever beheld occurred on US-84-285 outside Santa Fe, New Mexico, on Good Friday twenty years ago on a family vacation. It set in motion my awareness of *seekers* as I counted hundreds, maybe thousands, of Catholics from Indian, White, and Hispanic cultures walking north together, praying and reflecting, over twenty-six miles to El Santuario de Chimayo, a sacred church with healing dirt. Some started this annual pilgrimage from closer towns, but the striking image was the procession of halos of black hair and the white wooden crosses tilted on their backs. Regular people carrying crosses that looked made of pieces of painted snow fence. In the endless expanse of cerulean sky, I was transformed by their outward declaration of their following of Christ. Later, I found the lines of Psalm 119:45, "For all time and forever, I will walk freely in an open space, because I cherish your precepts."

I don't walk that freely. I think of myself as careful about revealing my beliefs, though it's no secret I value my relationship to God. I wear a silver Celtic cross on a chain around my neck that I never remove.

A tattoo of a Renaissance image of Mary cradling infant Jesus covers my upper left arm. But this isn't so much a declaration of faith as it is evidence I am afraid of people; the truth is, I put symbols on myself because I refuse to go into the world unprotected and unadorned.

I'm endlessly drawn to those who declare their love of God in front of others. It takes mettle. When I first joined a Franciscan church, I was (and still am) enthralled with the coarse brown robes and rope belts the friars and priests wear to honor St. Francis of Assisi, the Italian medieval saint who lived almost a thousand years ago. For that matter, I also love watching the communion line, though of course, that's less of a risk, being in a church, not wandering out in the world. I love the slow shuffle toward the chalice, the way some don't bother to fold their hands in prayer but just awkwardly let their long arms dangle and hang. I love how everyone receives their share, blessing themselves as the wafers melt in their mouths. It almost seems unreal to me, at times, that so many believe. It never fails to touch me when, at the end of Mass, the priest kisses the altar.

I carry what I believe inside me, not on my back. When I'm walking into my school, one arm loaded with books and lunch swinging from my other hand, you can't see the prayers swirling in my head as I buzz myself through the door: *I am surrounded by pure holy light.* Writing this book, now, I know these beliefs are moving from the internal. I am letting the words be seen, like fallen oak leaves under ice in winter, quiet and anonymous. Writing about faith is like melting ice, softening the barrier, and when that happens, the water is fresh and birds appear to drink and wash and swim. I love spring. Can I be more like spring in the world? Can I speak not just about love, but what *lives* within love?

The witnessing of the crosses on Holy Week stuck inside me, as has a magical trip I took to an Assisi artists' colony in 2016. I was attending

Mass in a tiny hillside church where St. Francis had also worshipped. A round woman in a white pleated dress entered and grabbed a long stick that had a fat binder clip tied to the end. She unclasped her fake white pearls, clipped them to the end of the stick, and lifted her beads high in the air to rub them all over a painting of the Madonna to (I guessed) bless them. She made sure that they touched every corner. Then she pulled the stick down, took her necklace back and placed it around her neck as Mass began. I was amazed at this gesture. I still think of that necklace. How cheap the beads were but once blessed, priceless.

I'm simply a seeker. That's all. On another blistering hot afternoon in Assisi, I descended the steps into the cool underground of the Basilica of St. Clare. I was unprepared for the intensity of the relics displayed. I became almost disoriented. Clare was lying there, a mummy, quite tiny. When I turned, I bumped into what I thought was a lantern, but was in fact a glass cube filled with snippets of baby-fine, white curls. This pile of her hair shook me even more than her bones. Beyond that, I encountered Francis's tunic, the primitive cloth roughly stitched. Maternal tenderness ran through me at the sight of his coarse stocking, only one, not even a pair. Blood crusted the arch—stains of the stigmata.

And that is when I saw Clare's dress.

The dress was the shade of spring, at the very beginning, when the tiniest of buds first appear in pale green mist. It floated high above all the other relics, as if airborne, so utterly, delightfully girly, I actually laughed out loud. I studied it for over an hour, because I didn't want to break the rules and photograph this sacred object. I needed to make sure the details were captured in my mind forever: the goddess-drape of the long sleeves, the high medieval bodice, the soft cotton, nearly see-through.

The next day, at breakfast with the other artists and writers, one of the women commented that she did not believe that dress could really be Clare's, after all these centuries. That it had to be some sort of reproduction, and besides, a dress that enormous would never have fit those small bones. I was appalled, then saddened, not arguing with her. I spent that day in silence under a ripening fig tree, thinking. And I have thought about this quite a bit ever since.

What I learned then is that I am a woman who quietly believes. I don't need to convince anyone of anything, I just need to follow the words of Psalm 119. "Your word is a lamp for my feet, a light for my path" (verse 105). And on this path, saints like Clare will keep leading me. I believe that dress *was* Clare's. I believe it was her feminine spirit that emanated from within. In the years since I stood before it, the dress has returned to me, lunar-moth like, floating in the dark and bringing coolness to the heat of my 3:00 a.m. insomnia. It reminds me to turn to Mary, to pray, to let go and let her magic fill the air like a lullaby. To let the Blessed Mother sing.

Psalm 139

I write frequently about being alone, loneliness, and the struggle of feeling separate. Some of the hardest moments are the times when the people closest to me don't even fully understand my life. Because the truth is, it's too much to expect that. Realistically, no one can *fully* understand your life. Not your mother, not your husband, not your child.

Recently this happened with my daughter when she called to wish me a happy birthday.

"Hey Mom, how do you feel?"

"I feel great."

"Well, that's good."

"Yeah, mostly I'm just glad to still be here. I'm grateful."

"That's a strange thing to say."

"What do you mean?"

"Of *course* you're still here."

I hesitated. My cancer lurks on my periphery and I want to be a good mother—should I bury it and protect or be vulnerable and share about it? "Dr. Vignati took out my cancer on my fiftieth birthday, so every birthday since then, it brings it all up. My birthday is very powerful for me. A lot of feelings."

"Oh, that's right. I forgot." She is a kind and compassionate woman. "Mom, I'm sorry."

"That's OK."

At first, I plummeted. My daughter is one of the people closest to me, and I understand that as my child, it would be painful to hold the fact of my cancer front and center. She *shouldn't* do that. She should live her life freely and openly, for herself. But it struck a nerve in that I was brought to that place of existential aloneness. Though my children, and others close to me, have supported me on my path, only God knows what it's like living with the diagnosis of Lynch Syndrome where the possibility of cancer returning, or a new one arriving, is strong.

I know my fear of dying is having a resurgence when I begin to obsess about what is right above my head in the attic. Living simply with no garage or basement to store unwanted and underused items, I own minimal furniture and don't collect much beyond ordinary items to keep a household going. But in the attic a mish-mash of boxes is stacked and I can't bear to think that I will make work for my children when they clean up after me after I die.

My daughter's tiny red shoes are up there. The memory of straightening the toe seam of her tights before slipping it on her foot. The overstuffed cardboard boxes of photo albums from when we were a family of four, the ivory pages now saffron.

I don't think only cancer survivors live with these sorts of thoughts, imagining a world empty of themselves, while their children grab armloads of the objects left behind. Regardless of circumstance, so many of us feel the inevitability of death as we stare into the dark and the dark stares right back.

In fact, only God knows what it's like for *any* of us moving through this world each in our own separate bodies.

I think of all the times I've tried to be there for friends and family whose lives have taken a desolate turn. I've never known which phrase is more accurate to offer as condolence. "I can't imagine what you are going through" is true. I can't imagine another's suffering. I feel this is a respectful thing to offer. But they're still alone, despite my being alongside them and offering empathy. I'll only reach so far into their situation. Sometimes I say, "I can *only* imagine what you are going through." Meaning, I can try and feel the contours of the details, put myself in your place, but I'm not *living* it. Three years ago when my son's closest friend Sunny died at the age of twenty-three, I could never understand my child's anguish at losing a friend he had since kindergarten. I could only watch. Watch the way the firelight of that endless winter did not touch the sunken shadows in my son's cheeks.

In each of our lives, we could fill lists of all the afflictions those near us have endured, waking up each day to put their feet onto the ground and begin walking that heartache again. We love them, we are there for them, we listen to them. But there is, always, that fundamental *alone*.

This is why Psalm 139 offers a comfort that I would characterize as mystical. The mystical is that which brings you right into the heart of God, and brings God right into the heart of *you*. Psalm 139 is, and always will be, a gorgeous piece of writing expressing the truth that not only does God know each of us, God has actually been alongside us, in ways no human being ever could, because it's beyond what any person can ever do. It's too much to ask. It's impossible.

I want to break it open, and then put it back together to show its wholeness. The psalm begins, "You have searched me and known me / you know when I lie down and when I sit up." (Some translations, such as the New King James Version, use *search*; others, *probe*.) So simple. Just in the act of sleeping and waking, we're befriended. It's not a feeling of being invaded by God, but accompanied, and encompassed. "Behind and before you encircle me" (Ps 139:5). The psalm covers both the years and the hours, our spoken words, everyday movements, our longings.

> If I take the wings of the dawn,
>> If I dwell in the remotest part of the sea,
> Even there your hand guides me.
> (139:9–10)

These lines burst with possibility. I can wake up to face another ordinary day, or I can *take the wings of dawn*. Such sweetness in that image. Even if I just disappear into the horizon of the ocean, even then, I won't be alone. Fantastically, this psalm moves from the landscape of the outer world to the truth of another globe we once floated in and filled: that world we briefly inhabited within our mothers.

> You formed me in my inmost being;
>> You knit me in my mother's womb.
> (139:13-14)

The use of the word *womb* is not new to many of us who've recited our lifetimes of Hail Marys with "blessed is the fruit of thy womb, Jesus." What I love is that this psalm takes us all the way back to when we first became. It reveres the beauty of our very beginnings and returns us to the miracle of our mothers. Even being carried within a womb, as each and every one of us was, God met us there. How many times have we heard, "You're born alone and you die alone"? Psalm 139 dispels this, assuring us that even before our birth, when we were being *woven, kneaded,* and *knitted,* we had a holy spirit paralleling us. Could there be anything more comforting than this belief, that we had this connection to God way back, starting within the cocoon of our own creation?

...not hidden from You,
   when I was made in secret.
(139:15)

Psalm 139 quells the unbearable state of separateness in these bodies in the world. To me, it's an astonishing work of art because it brings beauty, but it goes beyond even that. There's something particularly miraculous about this psalm that, upon each reading, brings with it refreshing succor. In one of my translations, it's labeled as addressing God's "omnipresence and omniscience"—massive words, and I appreciate their sweep. Another translation dials it down a bit, and reads "the All-knowing and Ever-present God." No matter the translation, no matter how close we are to others, no matter how much we *are* loved by our dearest friends and family, there will be times—often even years—when we're undeniably faced with the unique twists on our own singular paths. In my most fraught hours, I'm simply trying to find that inner friend—that *Anam Cara*—who's never ceased flowing alongside me. And I'll never fully know what the people I love most are going through, but this psalm is an aperture that widens, opening up the possibility that I can trust they have some*thing*, some*one*, alongside them. Because it's really hard, being human, and so alone.

Psalm 139
For the leader. A psalm of David.

I
Lord, you have probed me, you know me:
   you know when I sit and stand;
   you understand my thoughts from afar.
You sift through my travels and my rest;
   with all my ways you are familiar.
Even before a word is on my tongue,

Lord, you know it all.
Behind and before you encircle me
   and rest your hand upon me.
Such knowledge is too wonderful for me,
   far too lofty for me to reach.
Where can I go from your spirit?
   From your presence, where can I flee?
If I ascend to the heavens, you are there;
   if I lie down in Sheol, there you are.
If I take the wings of dawn
   and dwell beyond the sea,
Even there your hand guides me,
   your right hand holds me fast.
If I say, "Surely darkness shall hide me,
   and night shall be my light" —
Darkness is not dark for you,
   and night shines as the day.
Darkness and light are but one.

II
You formed my inmost being;
   you knit me in my mother's womb.
I praise you, because I am wonderfully made;
   wonderful are your works!
My very self you know.
My bones are not hidden from you,
   When I was being made in secret,
   fashioned in the depths of the earth.
Your eyes saw me unformed;
   in your book all are written down;
   my days were shaped, before one came to be.

III

How precious to me are your designs, O God;
   how vast the sum of them!
Were I to count them, they would outnumber the sands;
   when I complete them, still you are with me.
When you would destroy the wicked, O God,
   the bloodthirsty depart from me!
Your foes who conspire a plot against you
   are exalted in vain.

IV

Do I not hate, Lord, those who hate you?
Those who rise against you, do I not loathe?
With fierce hatred I hate them,
   enemies I count as my own.
Probe me, God, know my heart;
   try me, know my thoughts.
See if there is a wicked path in me;
lead me along an ancient path.

Order My Steps

I don't know how it took me decades to figure out that I have a stunningly terrible sense of direction. It was June of 2016, and I was standing all alone alongside a busy thoroughfare in ancient Rome, having walked in circles for two hours in the searing heat trying to find the church called St. Peter of the Chains, which held Michelangelo's sculpture *Moses.* The exhaust of passing taxis swirled my silk dress, and my feet in Mary Janes were on fire from the friction of the cobblestones.

While Italian streets can be tricky in both cities and towns, I suddenly realized that, even back home in New England, where I had lived for thirty-five years, I got lost almost everywhere I went. Most people seemed to have success getting places using a GPS. But even with a GPS, I still pulled swift U-turns. Highway signs come at me too fast and confuse me. I know arrows repeatedly warn of upcoming exits I'm supposed to take, but usually I sail past. Backtracking is just part of traveling, for me. I expect it. It doesn't help that I am also horrible at knowing measurements in feet and in miles. So when I am spoken to by my GPS guide, "Turn right in 700 feet," I usually don't.

It's no surprise, then, that my favorite cartoon as a kid was *Mr. Magoo,* the old man whose extreme nearsightedness left him in a perpetual state of going in the wrong direction. Because his eyes were so bad, he didn't even know that he was, in fact, forever being saved in the nick of time by some "coincidence." He thought, for example, he was driving on a lovely, sunny highway, when in fact he was high in the air on swinging steel construction girders of a skyscraper being built. It was stressful watching his constant state of peril. Yet Mr. Magoo was also perpetually being protected. Somehow, something was guiding him.

I still identify with Mr. Magoo's madcap crossings. In an odd way, perhaps being disoriented a lot of the time is a gift, because I can more fully understand the metaphor of needing God's help in my spiritual life to put my feet right. There is a perfect gospel song, "Order My Steps (In Your Word)." It's one of the most popular gospel songs in the world, with the title, from Psalm 119, repeating throughout, and the crescendo of the melody and harmony gets stuck in my head. *Order my steps in Your word.*

The psalms are the words to help in my own human state of being lost. These images recur throughout the Psalter.

The valiant one whose steps are guided by the Lord
(Ps 37:23)

He set my feet upon rock, steadies my steps
(Ps 40:2)

My steps have kept to your paths; my feet have not faltered
(Ps 17:5)

And my favorite:

He will not allow your foot to slip; or your guardian to sleep
(Ps 121: 3)

Maybe we are all lost and doing our best to help each other put one foot in front of the other. That day in Rome I eventually asked a bored Italian policeman how to get to the nearby Michelangelo, and he nodded in understanding and wrongly pointed me to "il Caravaggio." When at last I found it (I had been so close, and had not known), I collapsed nearby for hours to behold its beauty. Of the infinite treasures in Rome, I'd prioritized seeing this one because art historians posited that Michelangelo himself claimed this was his best work, of all the marble he spun from his genius, even better than the more famous *David*.

Within *San Pietro in Vincoli*, Moses is tense and poised and enormous, with peculiar horns on his head. This is because of a misunderstanding in translating the Hebrew word in the fourth century; apparently the words for "horn" and "shining" and "emitting rays" are very close. So instead of light, he has horns. I mention this because in my study of the psalms, translations of words can change perceptions. Can get thorny.

The signs in many languages read that if this sitting Moses stood up, he'd tower over us at thirteen feet high. Even with my challenges of distance and scale, I gasped at out how breathtakingly gigantic he would be. I didn't want to leave him, but eventually I had to. As I stepped into the scorched summer light, a musician was playing a jaunty "Let It Be" on his accordion for coins, and I was drawn toward it. I had no idea which way to go. I could only, once again, ask for help in ordering my steps to find my way back.

The Purple Heart

My father was a Marine, with Dress Blues that hung in the back of my parents' closet and his Purple Heart medals kept in the darkness of a velvet box in his handkerchief drawer. A veteran of the Korean War, my father served as a sharpshooter. He was wildly and admirably successful in the corporate world, yet emotionally detonated in our family, over and over, again and again. In my entire life, my father only referenced the war one time.

I remember the gloomy rain of that Sunday afternoon when I was in junior high. A classic black-and-white war movie was on the television. I said, "I hate war. There's no regard for human life."

He became very agitated. "Are you kidding me? The opposite is true. There's no more regard for human life than when you are sitting in a foxhole."

As his daughter, do those words help me understand the wildfire he held inside himself? That life meant the possibility of death, sudden death, always near? Is that what made him rage in all sorts of ways, physically and emotionally and threatening me with death from starvation and cold? One thing I do know from reading the psalms: that being a warrior can make you feel both completely unheard and unseen by God, and desperate for God's care. And so, in spite of the volatility of my childhood, every Sunday in his tie and dress shoes and business suit, after Mass, my father took a taper, touched it to a flickering wick, lit a fresh red votive candle, then knelt and prayed for the dead.

+ + +

I'm headed to Northampton to meet up with my old friend Doug Anderson to interview him. The hour on the highway helps me prepare, as I sort my memories of Doug into piles.

The very first time I crossed paths with Doug was when he was the mainstage reader at the prestigious Hillstead Museum Sunken Garden Poetry Festival. The Parrish-blue dusk became waxy and black. In the floodlights, he turned into a charcoal silhouette. His deep bass voice overtook the crowded lawns. As he read from his first poetry collection titled *The Moon Reflected Fire*, I remember the exact moment being pierced by something I never knew existed. And it was this: my entire life I had the longing to hear the truth of what it was to survive a war.

As a Vietnam Veteran, Doug has spent his life trying to articulate the truth of having been a medic in that war.

The poem he read that night in the garden was called "Purification." The narrator, "with blood still under my fingernails/from the last man who died in my arms," drinks from the breast of a young prostitute in Taiwan. This poem terrified me. I couldn't twist away from the straightforward language, how it existed beyond my idea of where a non-negotiable line of morality is drawn, and yet it was filled with the beauty of the human longing for maternal care. All I know is it brought me both relief in hearing a soldier unearth the truth, and nauseating terror in what was buried there. I consider myself pretty adept at analyzing literature, and I was stunned that I'd just heard one of the most moving war poems by an American poet in the twentieth century.

A few years after that reading, Doug and I and our spouses lived in the same neighborhood, and we all became close friends. Now Doug and I are each no longer married. His poem "Waiting For the Marriage Counselor" has a combination of images I love, from our previous domestic lives that did not last. *And the tomato / from your garden cut perfectly in half. / Our hands folded like birds waiting for the storm.*

I arrive to the college town of Northampton early: I've built in extra time in case I get temporarily lost, as I almost always do, even going to places I've been dozens of times. I wander in and out of the used bookstores and trinket shops until it's time for dinner. At five o'clock I enter Osaka, the restaurant Doug has chosen, and I recognize his bald head and white beard as he sits alone. He's in his mid-seventies now and crafts poignant poems about aging, but he still has a way of wrapping his arms around himself and leaning his elbows on the table so that his energy coils up, broadening his shoulders into those of a formidable young man.

We greet each other and settle into ordering. I know his face well, but his eyelids have changed into little triangles over his same cornflower blue eyes. He shares with me that last autumn he suffered two small strokes. I don't know what to say in response; I feel sad and scared. He still has his same intensity. I ask him to get whatever he wants, my treat, of course, and I match his order of Seafood Tempura and begin recording our conversation on my phone.

"I didn't read the questions you sent," he confesses. "It's been a rough week."

I had tried to prepare for our interview by emailing him some basic questions. I had to laugh. He's always had that bit of small defiance. He used to let my dog lick his barbecue dinner plate clean even though he knew it drove me crazy.

"It's okay, Doug." And it is. His poems have appeared in every major literary journal for decades, he's published three books of poetry and a memoir, and he's won prestigious awards, including grants from the National Endowment for the Arts, the McDowell Colony, and the Academy of American Poets. I tease him, "I mean, you do have the street cred of a Ph.D. in literature after all." I sip my green tea. "In thinking about the psalms, what came to mind for you?"

He blinks but holds my gaze. "They are *poems*. You can't separate the poetry from the spirituality. They carry the spirit, and by spirit I mean whatever is available for the person to get. Whatever is *touched* in the person to get."

Our food arrives. Two towers of fried deliciousness. Onion rings, crab legs, scallops. We take a few minutes to dig in.

"Did you ever seek out the psalms?"

He tightens his arms around himself. "Well, the 23rd, I've said to myself many times. 'Restoreth my soul'—how powerful is that? What does it mean to have your soul restored?"

"What does it mean to *you*?"

"It means living in the totality of myself, rather than having myself closed off by fear, or rage."

I think of when I first committed myself to the psalms out of the despair I feared would kill me if I didn't hold on tight. "That's so beautiful, Doug. So, especially for Psalm 23, is the shepherd your concept of God? A Higher Power?"

"Well, the shepherd knows exactly how *many* sheep there are. He knows exactly where they are at all times. He knows immediately if one has strayed. He knows their reactions to predators. A shepherd is someone with a high degree of *awareness*."

I've never once considered the specifics of a shepherd's *skills*, and I find this description of God incredibly uplifting.

He continues. "Jesus allows for a personal relationship with all that is human. He would accept whatever condition I am in, without judgment. This is how I see him. He could forgive his tormentors and understand them."

I ask, "If you have a concept of a Higher Power—or God—what language are you comfortable with in that? God, Jesus, Christ, Holy Spirit, what words are you comfortable with?

"All of those," he says, and then adds, "Mohammed."

"Was there ever a pivot in your life?"

"Yes. My mother started going to an Episcopal church when I was in high school. I now understand I had depression. My mother suggested I go see Ferguson. He wrote a book on Christian theology. I went to talk to him. At a certain point I felt something pouring into me. We were just chatting. I felt it enter me, like an amphetamine, long before I knew what that was. He looked at me and said, 'Right now I am giving you an injection of spirit.' And I've never been able to explain that experience. I don't tell this to very many people."

I flash to my experience with Jesus in a hospital room. I was two months pregnant with my son when my grandmother lay dying in 1992. I never told anyone that story of Jesus for ten years. I kept it inside. I didn't want to sully it; to this day, I rarely speak of it. The last time I let it surface, it was six years ago during a raw conversation with my son where all sorts of truths came tumbling out. Now, I don't want to intrude on Doug's private world.

I ask, "Is it okay that I record this?"

He doesn't hesitate. "Yep."

I feel honored in his willingness to share this experience.

"And when I did tell people, they scoffed. And I've always wanted to get back to that, whatever it was. But I haven't been able to."

"Really?"

"Yeah. It didn't direct my life very well. I became very lost and alcoholic. All of these things you would not expect to have happen after having had an injection of spirit. This was irrational and indescribable. The only way I can approach the memory is to go into non-knowing. I do think it left the door open for a kind of spirituality."

"You were how old?

"Sixteen."

"Do you think this memory might have sustained you?"

"I know there is something you can return to. The Sufis talk about remembering who you really are."

I remember in Italy at La Cella, where St. Francis once lived, a sign that read *Stop in Silence Before God, Rediscover Who You Are.* "To me, Psalm 23 has such a sense of returning. You're saying there's this beautiful level you always carried, even if you couldn't access it."

"It was there to have it."

We focus on devouring our meals for a few minutes. The fried crust of the briny seafood is sweet. Wiping the flakes off my fingers, the grease stains the napkin. "Do you remember any specific time when you sought Psalm 23?"

Doug's language suddenly changes from the unfurling, cadenced sentences of a professor to the chopped-up words of the medic. "Vietnam. Terrified. Terrified."

We both go silent. I look into his eyes as he drops into another place inside himself, travels somewhere else within. "There's so many other lines in that psalm. There is the spiritual food. One of the things that fear does, and anger does, is to shut down all the refined human capabilities. So in offering this sumptuous meal, the banquet, which is really life, which is really all the wonderful things in life, it's a form of restoration. 'Thou preparest a table in the sight of my enemies.' Here you have a man being hunted. Surrounded by danger. Suddenly able to eat. How many people do you know who can eat when they are afraid?"

I think of all the women I know with disordered eating. I think of my own eating disorder when I was a teen. All of the ways that being a woman makes you afraid.

"It's funny, in Vietnam, a lot of guys got very macho in order to handle their fear—and it never worked, and some of the things scrawled on the backs of flap jackets—one of them which cracks me up every time I think of it is 'Though I walk through the valley of the shadow of death, I will fear no evil because I am the biggest badass in the valley.'"

I picture these words in a childish chicken-scratch, the handwriting of a son.

He adds, "That's of course humorous. But this is someone who believes that shutting down the heart will keep you alive. And in a sense, he may be right. Because you shut down anything like tenderness in those situations."

"Did you have a copy of Psalm 23, or did you have it memorized?"

"I had it memorized. I had a terrible time the first two years of sobriety. I turned to it then. Everything I attempted to bury about my life was staring me in the face."

"How long have you been sober now?"

"Thirty-two years."

My meal is barely half-eaten, yet I'm full, and my satiation makes me a bit dreamy. "My research keeps pointing out the fact that Jesus sang the psalms. That you know, culturally, he would have. Everyone did. The thought of him singing Psalm 23 is so beautiful I cannot stand it." Saying this emboldens me to probe. I take a risk. "You used the word *tormentors*."

He nods and quotes Jesus on the cross. "'They know not what they do.'"

"Did you take that inside your heart?"

He answers, "Yeah. Yeah," in a chippy tone. Then he softens. "For many of us, more veterans than are acknowledged, it opened up a curiosity about our enemy. And it was magnetizing to want to know who they were, these people who would fight so hard, and die in such numbers, with such little equipment compared to us, and eating a bag of rice a day. What drives someone like this? Who were they? What was the spirit that drove them to fight with such ferocity against planes, rockets?

"In the last half century since the war, I've gone back twice. I know many of my former enemies, particularly poets and fiction writers, and have listened to them, and we've exchanged stories of what it was like, become friends. For many years I was involved with the Joiner Center for the Study of War and Its Social Consequences, begun by veterans who felt something was really incomplete after their experience with the war. They had a hunger, a longing, to know more about the country they fought against. And the people they fought."

"Is there a possibility that poetry allowed for deeper forgiveness?"

"Yes. It allowed for deeper connection. You can't write poetry with a closed heart. We reached out; they reached back."

A long pause between us. I think of David's vulnerability in telling God how he feels.

I ask, "Do you think that David was in the same situation as you guys?"

"Yes."

"A poet—"

Doug tightens his arms around himself and his shoulders lift and widen. "Clearly."

My voice goes serious. "—exposed to extraordinary violence, stress, harassment, slander, everything, and yet David kept reaching out to

God, trusting that God would reach back. Were you surprised you had that sort of reach in you?"

"I knew I had a longing."

This is one thing I know about. "Like a deer longs for water." Then, unexpectedly, I feel the real reason I am bonded to Doug begin to bubble inside me. I try and quell it.

He notices my shift. "You doing okay over there?"

"I'm doing great." I force myself to sound upbeat, but can't keep it going. I falter, not making sense. "I'm sure you're right, you know your journey. I will say that, you know, when—" It comes flooding back. "You would stop by my house when I had cancer, and you never once overstayed your visit by one minute. You would stay for ten minutes. Sometime twenty. You'd just listen and then take your leave so gently."

I'm the one who now disappears into the past of my dilapidated green couch, of my TV room. I had a husband then, an intact family, a home. The lamplight had shone behind Doug's head. I recall the exact texture of the stretched-out fabric of the gauchos I wore every day and the fit of my daughter's green Lesley University sweatshirt.

It had been nine years since they pulled my intestines from my body and cut the cancer out. I had been gutted like a fish. I received tremendous love and support, meals left on the porch, lilies. "You would just listen to me, and I felt free to say what was in my heart, all that fear and sorrow and gratitude, and not feel the burden of worrying—about— you never stayed that long, it was very respectful, you never made it about you, you never said anything about yourself, it was always like, 'Okay Maureen, just talk, don't hold back,' and it was such a gift to be heard like that." I dab my tears with my greasy napkin.

Doug nods. "It's good to just shut up and listen. Somehow just let the person know they've been heard."

This is what the psalms are to me. Two things happening at once. The act of speaking. The act of being listened to.

Our waitress begins to pack up my leftovers. "Would you like the rice?"

I nod.

Doug says one more thing before we leave. "Look at Psalm 139, the role of light and dark. One offsets the other, light in darkness, and darkness in light."

We head toward his car. "Did you get enough to eat?" I ask. I've always felt a maternal care toward Doug, wanting him to be okay.

"Sure. Yes."

"And what about your orthotics? When I saw you last summer, you were in pain, waiting for them."

"They're good. I'm much better."

He shows me his new used car, a Rav 4, and we make small talk about that for a while, and when I hug him goodbye, I remember to tell him, "Oh, Madeline said to say hello." I don't want to part, because I don't know when, or if, I will ever see Doug again.

I set my GPS for home, craving the illumination and speed of the highway to once again clear my head. I'll roll all the windows down and blast Tom Petty and the Heartbreakers. But as usual, I take wrong turns even in spite of my navigational support, and soon I realize I'm far from Route 91 and instead I'm taking the slow back way. No highway, only traffic lights and the shuttered up stores of the main streets linking the towns of Massachusetts, over the border into Connecticut.

Again and again, how many times do we glide through darkness trying to find our way home?

What Remains

The woods along the Farmington River are clear and quiet, except for my own footsteps on the icy gravel. The overlap of branches, the thatch of it all, and then one lone woodpecker fills the air with tapping into bark, the puncture of a rotting trunk. Pure silence, even more pronounced, when the woodpecker is gone. I was enraged when I first beheld what the hard-hatted workers in green fluorescent vests had done this past year to these woods to build the new bridge at the end of Old Farms Road. My first thoughts were, *Oh my God, they raped it.* Thousands of old trees were decimated, their tree-trunk bodies swept away, leaving ugly acres of amputated stumps.

But astonishingly, as they bulldozed, they found evidence of people having lived here 12,000 years ago. This stunning revelation has become the oldest and largest cache of artifacts — 15,000 — that's ever been found in all of Southern New England. The poet in me is intoxicated by this finding, that these ancient people of the Paleoindian Period ate water lilies, left behind jewelry, ate turtles (like the ones sunning themselves in summer on fallen lake-logs), and that during their time — and I can barely get my mind around this — mammoths existed.

"Modern life," "suburban crawl," the rising population, whatever we call it, pushes us into secular places where land is ripped apart and the pieces are discarded with no sense of attachment. But pieces returned, unearthed, providing such a sense of wonder that these Native Americans walked on this exact land over 12,000 years ago. I'm breathless imagining who moved through this forest. People have been the same throughout time; I sense the shy boys and girls, way back, growing up, growing older, becoming lovers, time passing, their children shrieking through the vines. This valley is idyllic even *with* the encroaching prefab housing developments and generic strip malls, but it must have been so peacefully tranquil and perfect back then. One thing I'm certain of: Whoever these people were, they loved this flowing river as fiercely as I do. I feel connected to them in this love.

The beauty of being human is to turn to our spiritual ancestors, to cherish what they left behind, what remains. What *has* lasted? What has endured? Where can we turn for anything permanent when our loves, and our lives, are so exquisitely and heartbreakingly *imperma-nent?* Something is shifting in me, very far inside, as I am turning to these old psalms, reading them every day. I am starting to believe, throughout these millenniums, there's been something unfailing and steadfast. And I think it might be God.

A Hard Day's Night

What if one of the most admired and revered chords *ever* constructed was destroyed and we could never hear it again? If I could insert an actual sound here, I'd cut and paste the opening chord to the Beatles "A Hard Day's Night." Perhaps you can hear the vibrations in your head, as I do. I love to play this chord over and over. It breaks right in.

The three seconds of sound is considered one of the most innovative, influential, and spectacular chords ever recorded. Mathematicians have burrowed into it, musicians have dismantled and examined the pieces like an engine to figure out how the harmony—almost at the brink of *dis*harmony—soars, intricate and luminous. I'm using this chord as a simple example to mourn the fact that all the ancient music of the psalms is lost. We have no idea what that music was.

Yes, all of the original music is gone. The poems are what remain. I'm certain the music was beautiful because some of the missing melodies have titles listed at the beginning of some psalms, but they're melodies we'll never hear. What would a song called "Do Not Destroy" sound like, as the notes of Psalm 59 read? It must have been an unbearable ache, the melody called *The deer of the dawn*, the notes woven with "My God, my God, why have you abandoned me?" (Ps 22:2).

I want to hear the melody titled *Lilies* (Ps 60) woven with the lament "I am weary with crying out." But it's extinct. If I stay very still and meditate on it, I sense the song of "Lilies" on the edge of my heart, a vibration, like when the bells of a faint Ave Maria ring in a valley and by the time you stop to really listen, they're gone, and you wonder if you even heard it at all.

We don't even know if *Upon the Gittith* (Ps 8) means a melody or an instrument. Other mysteries that you come upon in the psalms are found in tiny fonts; in many translations, the word *Selah* appears seventy-one times. Sometimes it's at the end of a numbered section; other times it's in the middle of a stanza. Pronounced *Sea*-la, even the scholars aren't sure exactly what this melodious word means; it might translate as "interlude." If the scholars who have devoted their waking hours to figuring out these poems don't know, then it's an example of how all seekers—the newcomers and the veterans—can find unlimited interpretations as they enter them.

The words are intact. We should celebrate how they've carried and clutched through the centuries. The music is back there, but we can't return to find it. Whatever it was, it's gone, like so many things in our lives we cannot return to, memories, now inaudible, in a desert, paused on mute.

The Place Where the Light Enters You

Today the sun is aimed at a rare angle on the western horizon, shooting all the way through the narrow window across my dining room into the galley kitchen, and landing on the counter with the wide, flat bowls on top of the microwave. The bowls are empty. No bread and ripening fruit. One bowl is painted with a pair of country rabbits and the other's glazed with maroon and blue iris with a serrated chip in the edge. I don't want to throw it out and replace it; it has sentimental value because my dear friend Vicki gave it to me years ago.

The bowls are overflowing with light. The sun only finds that corner for a few days of the entire year, and for few minutes in these days. That's it. I want to pay attention so much to this life that when the elusive light comes to my ordinary home, I stop and dip myself in it. Just as the poet Rumi declares, "The wound is the place where the light enters you." During those two years of pain, and the seventeen holes in my body, I hung on to that idea of light getting inside me. This changed me, permanently, into a devotee of light. In the time it took to write this down and describe it, the corner of the kitchen is gray again.

The bowls hold shadows. Nothing lasts. Except—

Except the desire for a love everlasting, for love everlasting, for ever-lasting love.

Violence

I've gone around and around, trying to figure out how to begin to talk about the violence. I isolated words from Psalm 58 to give a sort of slow-pitch: *brambles and thistles*. But the violence of the psalms is far beyond something that grows wild and pierces you. I've become fiercely protective, and I keep imagining a reader giving them a brief chance and being repelled by the brutality, rejecting them outright because there hasn't been a bridge to create an understanding.

When we turn to prayer, we want relief, but if you open the psalms for "pretty," you will not be satisfied. Because they're deeper than pretty. If I had to explain them in the fewest words possible, it would be the ending of John Keats' "Ode on a Grecian Urn": "Beauty is truth, truth beauty,—that is all/ Ye know on earth, and all ye need to know." With the closing lines of that masterpiece from the English Romantic poet, we can traverse the psalms' violence as an exploration of the *truth* of what it is to be human. All over our planet and throughout every century, to varying degrees, hasn't every single human being been exposed to violence? Both coming from outside, and from within?

The entire sweep of all one hundred and fifty poems explores the crosshatch of our emotions, including the repeated outrage. The psalms were written at a time of tribal wars; since there was no real belief in an afterlife where some sort of justice might be attained, it was imperative that God be just. The desire for both revenge and fairness, intertwined, runs throughout. So it helps to understand that in context. There's much history to learn to let the poems heal us today, and I have a long way to go in this area. Psalm 58 goes right to the desire to see those who've hurt us suffer, wishing they would "wither," and disappear. The juxtaposition of a dissolving snail with a miscarriage never fails to astound me.

Psalm 58

Do you indeed pronounce justice, O gods;
　do you judge fairly you children of Adam?
No, you freely engage in crime;
　your hands dispense violence to the earth.

II

The wicked have been corrupt since birth;
　liars from the womb, they have gone astray.
Their venom is like the venom of a snake,
　like that of a serpent stopping its ears,
So as not to hear the voice of the charmer
　or the enchanter with cunning spells.

III

O God, smash the teeth in their mouths;
　break the fangs of these lions, Lord!
Make them vanish like water flowing away;
　trodden down, let them wither like grass.
Let them dissolve like a snail that oozes away,
　like an untimely birth that never sees the sun.

Suddenly, like brambles or thistles,

have the whirlwind snatch them away.
Then the just shall rejoice to see the vengeance
    and bathe their feet in the blood of the wicked.
Then people will say:
"Truly there is a reward for the just;
    there is a God who is judge on earth!"

When I first began writing on the psalms, I knew that it wasn't going to be something I "did" at certain times, separate from my other obligations and duties. I knew they'd begin to seep into my life, but I didn't know how. Very swiftly, I learned an illustrative lesson from Andre.

I have taught creative writing to teens in Hartford for twenty-four years at an arts magnet high school, a diverse environment where kids immerse themselves in the arts while getting all their core academic subjects. We'd just switched semesters two weeks prior, and I had a new roster. I didn't know him very well yet, but I already figured out that Andre was a big personality with a great flare for expression. He burst into the room at the start of class.

"I wanna punch her in the face," he growled, and swung his backpack up into the air so that it landed with a wallop on the table.

I let the rest of the students settle in, and then I took a big breath. As a writing teacher, it's my job to provide a mirror, and a space, for the emotions that live inside us. "Let's talk about this. Remember my guiding philosophy? From the poet Hafiz? 'What we speak becomes the house we live in.' Who here has ever said they want to punch someone? Or slap someone?"

A hush came over the room. They all kept their elbows tight to their bodies, but turned their palms toward me in a shy show of hands. If there's one thing adolescents love, deserve, and need, it's uninterrupted time—together with their peers—to tell the truth about what they feel.

I wanted them to reflect on the words that surrounded them. "How many times a day at this school do you hear that someone wants to punch someone? How many times do you hear 'I want to smack her'?"

Dessaray gave a sad little grin. "All day. A lot."

"We have no way of knowing how that affects your education. Hearing that all day." I thought of how lockdowns had to also be driving their collective aggression, the grotesque reality we all lived with in a classroom together. As a public school teacher, my colleagues and I have had to prepare for the possibility of a murderous school shooter coming into our classroom firing an AK-47. We have practiced shutting the blinds. Turning out the lights. Locking the door then barricading it with a bookcase and following our training of not opening the door even if the loudspeaker says "ALL CLEAR" because it could be a perpetrator getting us to be easier targets if we let him in.

"I say it," Andre offered, "because I just feel so hot sometimes. So full of hate. I feel better after I say it. It explodes out of me."

From inside a folder I pulled out a stack of copies of Byron Katie's Emotion List and passed them out. It contains the most detailed emotion list I've ever encountered, and I use it all the time in all my classes. Dozens and dozens of emotions are listed by simpler headings like *angry, hurt, sad, happy, alive*. But the list is more precise: *scornful, miffed, forlorn, sunny, courageous*. "Pick four things that you are feeling," I instructed. In order to get them to write from the heart, I try to guide them within. They spend many hours of the day sighing with their eyes turned to the side, watching the clock, waiting for lunch or for dismissal, dutifully reaching for their dulled pencils, or losing themselves in their cell phones.

When I opened up the discussion to the group, I asked Andre if he wanted to share or keep his insights private.

"I'll go." He brightened. "My words are *disappointed, rejected, radiant,* and *fragile*."

My heart broke open. This hulking man-child who entered my class wanting to punch one of my colleagues in the face was telling us that underneath the hurt, he's both radiant and fragile.

I dovetailed into my lesson plan for the day, and they each selected a photograph to write about. From my stack, Andre chose a close-up of shell-pink zinnias growing along a broken Hartford sidewalk. I set the timer for ten minutes, and they quietly filled a page in their journals. He waved me over to read his poem about how seeds were planted, titled "Flowers of Friendship." He wanted to share it but was overcome with shyness.

He asked me to read it for him. With his wide brown knuckles pointing toward us, Andre clutched the photo in front of his face. We laughed; he had given himself a face of sunlit petals. When I read aloud to my students, I speak slowly, intentionally, and I felt his radiance. Their expressions softened as we listened. Especially Dessaray's. I read his last line:

"Then, when the flowers come, you know you are ready for the world."

A long silence as it sank in. The kids burst into gentle applause. Like a psalm that pivots from anger and anguish to joy, Andre, in true Davidic fashion, no longer lost and rejected, stood up and began to swirl his fists in a dance. The smiles from his peers egged him on.

+ + +

I am headed, still, into scary territory and want to begin with the first and last lines of a poem by the great Black poet Langston Hughes, written when he was a teenager: "I've known rivers, ancient dusky rivers" and "My soul has grown deep like the rivers."

I've known rivers too, but I've known violence as well.

In my perfect world I'd keep danger and terror separate from the flow of the natural beauty, but that's not how life is constructed. I feel sickened thinking about this directly, as I prefer to write about my sanctuaries as being untouched, and untouchable. This includes my home, my school, my meadows, my church. Who hasn't yearned to feel safe here on this earth? And yet, where is there a place of safety *guaranteed* to stay safe? It doesn't exist. I could fill pages with sudden random acts of violence—the result of misogyny, racism, intolerance, mental illness—that have caused unspeakable, and intergenerational, suffering and pain. This is one of the hardest parts of the human condition. "Listen to my cry for help, for I am brought very low, Rescue me from my pursuers, for they are too strong for me" (Ps 142:7).

Last spring, just as an old turtle had climbed the muddy bank of the river and scraped a divot with her back legs to lay eggs, a local news van rushed up to me. I was the only one walking; the SUVs of the parents had left the soccer field parking lot as the sun began to set. A reporter jumped out of the van.

"May we talk with you?"

I hesitated. I'd never seen a reporter here, ever. "About?"

He named the woman who had recently gone missing. Her name was all over the state and national headlines. They were dredging the pond a few acres north of where we stood because law enforcement believed her husband may have killed her and dumped her body there along the water-skiing ramps.

"Does this make you more wary, more afraid of being here?" He pointed the microphone at me and his assistant with the camera on his shoulder began to record.

I thought of the roads I used to walk, at a reservoir ten miles away, where a woman named Agnieszka had been shot in broad daylight. They only recently, after twenty-two years, are getting closer to arresting her murderer. I remembered how I read that her father had died shortly after that, carried away, drowned by a wave in Rhode Island. In the other direction from the river, a woman jogger had been stabbed on the bike trail, and it took four years to figure out who did it. "No. Nowhere is really safe," I said.

They asked me to spell my first and last name, thanked me, and left. The body of the woman was not found in the nearby pond, though her blood was found in trashcans on sponges along Route 44 in the city nearby, and her husband was arrested as a suspect. Recently, he took his own life, leaving their five children orphans.

To walk in the woods to find that peace that nature brings, in every season, is to know risk. *Do you go there alone?* The most devastating poem about this relentless dread is written by Marge Piercy. To read her "Rape Poem" is to look directly at the fear that a woman walking alone never stops carrying.

+ + +

If you have wanted to give up…

As I have wanted to give up…

I offer this: "Truth shall spring up like the water from the earth, justice shall rain from the heavens" (Ps 85:11). This is the translation from the missalette. I don't know what version it is, but it's how the cantor sang it. I hung on to these words, and they got me through the hardest time in my life. I was thirty-five. I lived by those words for a long time, and this was the very first time the psalms sought me out and found me.

I could envision it clearly. How truth would be flowing so clear I'd be able to drink directly from it.

A stream with a shaded embankment of bursting blue forget-me-nots.

Then justice would rain.

A warm summer sun-shower.

Barefoot kids running everywhere, laughing and shrieking.

Puddles. In flattened blades of grass. On sidewalks and driveway pavement.

A free-for all of innocence, the world safe and sopping.

I lived in a more populated city then. Every day I walked by a tennis court, and right where the chain-link poked out like barbed wire, I wished I was no longer alive. I knew my family was depending on me, so in the despair, I'd ask for help. I knew I was on the edge. When that feeling ensnared me, I'd whisper, *Jesus, help me.* And the words would come to me, "Truth shall spring up like the waters from the earth, justice shall rain from the heavens." They found me again and again. I'd hear them as a song, with the melody, and I'd see the pattern of the black notes like it appeared in the missalette. They gave me hope. When those words came looking for me, they didn't give up. I didn't sing them though, not then. Instead they made my throat close up, blocking a song when I tried.

Tears in a Flask

"My wanderings you have noted; are my tears not stored in your flask, recorded in your book?" (Ps 56:9). This idea undoes me. All the tears I shed my first winter divorced after twenty-five years of marriage, now alone. My new house had a gas fireplace. Every bluing dawn I awoke, went downstairs with my journal, and clicked the little black remote on the hearth. It beeped, then had a moment of nothing, then a whooshing sound proceeded a warming orange and yellow in the center of fake logs. My tears came fast and hard alongside the full fanning open of the flames. My journals from that time, 8 x 14 white legal pads with no covers, just backs of cardboard, are warped as if having been left too near an open window, unprotected from rain. I never even knew a human being could make so many tears. I must have filled that flask to the brim.

The idea that God saved all those tears is a deeply paternal and maternal one. Parents save the precious representations of their children. On my dining room wall to the left is a pencil drawing of a... actually, I don't know what it is, other than a Star Wars character flying on a machine. Is it flying in air or riding sand across the desert? I don't know. This drawing my son made twenty years ago is my way of holding on to the little boy he was.

The same theme returns: God doesn't leave us when sorrow bends our spines. I can trust a God who doesn't rush us but, by allowing our emotions to unfold and to pass, guides us to peace.

We ourselves are a landscape, with both tears and love flowing through. When I picture a tear that God catches, it's like a raindrop wiggling at the tip of a pine bough, and for the briefest moment, it becomes a dazzling prism, exploding with a pure ruby red, violet, then green. It falls with a renewed brightness, into "the light of the living" (Ps 56:14).

The Overwhelming, Never-Ending, Reckless Love of God

I hesitate to tell this story, because I don't want sweet, fierce Phaedra to be judged. She was a student of mine who, several years back, blurted out suddenly in class, "Maureen, what is it like to give birth?" We all cracked up at how random the question was during a discussion of an e.e. cummings poem. I delicately worked to evade the question. I've been teaching teen girls a long time, and they never *really* want to know what birth is like. Within weeks, I found out that Phaedra was pregnant. Even before that, she had a roundness to her face and softness to her body that was somehow motherly.

When she told her mother, her mother went ballistic. Phaedra's mother had had her when she was very young, and she was afraid for the struggle that Phaedra was facing. I wasn't there, of course, but Phaedra told me of the emotional storm that raged for days. Their lives went on, but they were at odds, arguing and screaming. Then, one night, Phaedra and her mother were in a car together parked outside and it began to rain really hard. They were listening to K-LOVE, the contemporary Christian music station. A song came on that shifted her mother from fury to sadness and fear. Phaedra's mother said she would do whatever she could to help her daughter (and she has) but that Phaedra needed to understand that the hardship would be relentless.

"We were bawling our heads off," Phaedra told me later, laughing, "Just sitting there listening to dumb old K-LOVE."

I shook my head in understanding. I had also been reduced to tears listening to that station. The music is mostly bland and commercial, the refrains often corny.

"Yup." She spoke the lyrics that had connected them: "It's the overwhelming, never-ending, reckless love of God."

I actually love the sweep of those words, and I love that song. It broke through, like the neon spire atop St. Joseph Cathedral shining through gloomy late afternoons and making the dark five o'clock nights of November Daylight Savings that much easier to bear. Around the time of this song's release, there was a conflict, covered in the media, about whether or not the word *reckless* was "Christian" in describing God. As an educator I believe in discourse, discussion. But Christians can go after each other with venom, arrogance, spite — it's exhausting.

Catholics go after one another as well. We know the issues that most divide us. I don't even want to say them here. It can be an endless game of one-upmanship, hurling Scripture around for points. It leads to the worst thing of all: a cynicism that drains us of what we need most — hope. I remember a couple years back, my mother said to me, "I never knew you had such a backbone of steel." Meaning, I'm strong. Though she and I don't talk about God, I know it was my faith that guided me. But even with my powerful longings for the Divine, there are times all the divisions and misunderstandings toward and between religions just make me want to put my hands in my coat pockets, push out the doors of the brick-and-mortar church, and brace myself for the cold grit in life's winds all alone.

+ + +

I was raised in the Catholic Church by a father who took us to Mass every week. My mother was Protestant and never went a single Sunday, though she did attend when we made sacraments. My little brother and older sister and I used to question this constantly as we rushed around on Sunday mornings trying to not be late (we were *always* late).

"Mommy, why don't you have to go?"

She would just shrug, very noncommittally.

"It's not fair!" we'd shout as we ran out the back door.

We used to play a game, when we returned home from Mass. We'd sprint from my father's car to see who could tag our mother first. She was always still in her blue forget-me-nots robe.

My mother took us to CCD classes. She bought our elaborate Easter outfits. When my father was out of town, she still took us to church and dropped us off. She tried hard, and did an incredible job, raising us in a faith to which she had no connection. My mother's heart, her spiritual heart, is in the wonders of August sunsets on Maine's lakeshore, night's loons calling. But she did her darndest to help us follow the Catholic rules. My siblings and I used to deliberately drive her crazy by taking the round bread-and-butter pickles out of our baloney sandwiches and giving them to each other like priests giving communion wafers, saying, "The Body of Christ."

"Stop it!" she'd say, squashing it swiftly.

Not once did my mother say anything derogatory, mocking, or snide about Catholicism. She was neither superior to it, nor inferior. And my father never once said anything about my mom being a different religion than the four of us. It was a non-issue. In fact, she has no religion at all. And yet, her connection to nature is as holy as David's in the psalms.

I think of the rain drumming on that car with Phaedra and her mother, of the song drawing them together, of Phaedra's little boy being born, of my own mother marrying my father when she was a teenager, having my sister when she was nineteen. I think of how exhausting all the walls and divisions are between faiths. What name people call their God. Who's saved and who isn't. Who believes the right thing and who doesn't. Who's worthy, who's a screw-up, who's a saint. All I know is: My mother, for her entire life, has sought to have her heart in the right place. How many people can claim that?

The Mary Cassatts

I hear so many stories of how people raised in the faith have left the Church, how the generation of young people in their twenties and thirties don't seek out religion; I hear percentages. And I understand the multitude of reasons for it. For starters, no one can ever measure the impact of the sexual abuse scandals that rotted the roots of the Church. I sometimes have suspicions and fears of the clergy, that's the truth. I've thought about this for many years, wondering why I still go. It's because, in certain churches, my cynicism washes away, my heart opens, and I feel something surrounding me. I realize this is a strong word, but it's the one I need: I often feel something holy.

It happened yesterday. A woman, nearing her confirmation, was asked to come to the altar for the congregation to offer her support as she neared the end, or rather the beginning, of her journey. Perhaps based on all the press of people leaving the Church, I always perk up with curiosity when I see adults converting. Father Tom looked around our boisterous 10:00 a.m. family Mass. A long pause created suspense as we all waited for her to emerge. Where was she?

She suddenly stepped into clear view, carefully climbing the marble steps in her heels, stopping, then turning toward us. We gasped at the beauty of this mother carrying an infant in her arms. I think she was

Filipino, with glossy black hair cascading down her back ending in curls. She wore a pink headband sparkling with delicate silver flowers.

Father Tom asked us to pray for her. As she received the blessings, the baby in her arms reached out and touched the mother's face with a tenderness exactly like a charcoal by Mary Cassatt. The baby reached with control, not recklessly waving her fist, not tapping her mother's face, not patting it, but a complete and full perfect reach, placing a tiny hand upon her mother's cheek. The mother's confirmation sponsor answered the questions about what a good job the mother had been doing in her footsteps toward becoming Catholic. The child kept her open hand upon the mother's face as they gazed into each other's eyes. The mother's face glowed with a slight smile, and I think if she hadn't had so many strangers staring at her, she would have really let go into the bond of being with her baby. It's not as if she was holding back, exactly; it's that the mother was in the spotlight, and shy. I shifted and beheld the pews to the right of me, every row, filled with people who had broken into smiles, faces beaming.

We held that Madonna and Child image as we sang a bit louder than usual, and exited, shaking hands in greeting with Father Cyd and Father John waiting outside with wool caps on their shaved heads, then the plains of the parking lot emptying, the vast expanse of sky, the rushing sound of the highway, the bent homeless man by the exit who plays his out-of-tune harmonica for coins after Mass, one leg lifted and his spine curved like a Kokopelli, his song carried off like cinders tinting the wind.

Merton

I do not mean this to offend, but it seems to me we are smitten, yes, we are a bit *in love*, with Thomas Merton.

In a recent meeting of the Central Connecticut Thomas Merton Society, I joined a bunch of tenderhearted, unpretentious seekers in jeans sitting in a small circle of chairs in a classroom at Holy Family Monastery. We were watching a documentary about the extraordinary sweep of Merton's life as a monk and a writer. Considered to be the most essential Catholic writer of the twentieth century, there was grainy footage of him giving an eloquent speech: "This idea of abandoning yourself to God and going off where God leads you..." He stepped down from the podium and asked, "Can I get a Coke?" It was the final footage of him, as he died in a freak accident a few days later. During our discussion of this moment, despite the morbid overtones, we laughed at what an ordinary guy Merton—considered by many to be a mystic—could be. A man offered, "He's an enigma."

Yes, an enigma. That's the truest statement about Merton, and one with which I am pretty sure Merton, in all his humility, would disagree. He's been gone fifty years, leaving behind sixty books for us to hold and peer into. It's been nearly impossible for me to catch up to him for long; he always seems to dart away again. At best, I have understood, perhaps, a few paragraphs, and a few prayers. Many devoted scholars—and many regular people—have gotten much closer than I ever will in grasping him. I did, however, recently encounter a body of his visual work that spiritually stunned me—and reinforced my lifelong commitment to reading and following him.

As for the dashing animus figure he represents, I've heard it posited that enlightened people have a certain attractive aura. Not romantic, necessarily, but a way of pulling you toward them. You find this with photos of Merton. Most feature the curve of his bald head (though my favorite is him in a wool cap, white monk robes, and a jean jacket). He has two distinct expressions. One is more serious, catching him glancing to the side, moving through his own internal stone wall, his own willow, the place of being free and all alone as the contemplative that he was.

But other photos, when he looks out into the world, he grins right at the camera, he has what can only be described as an impish expression. His dark eyes have distinct crow's feet, deep lines, and his slight smile is curved with a delight that veers to mischievous. I guess you could classify him as handsome, but it's beyond that. You can feel how absolutely in the moment he was, and how being so present filled him up. And it just draws you in and makes you want to feel that grounded too. It makes you want to be that happy, being earthbound.

I first was exposed to Merton at Ithaca College with my teacher George Clarkson. George, a grandfather figure for all of us, was one of the gentlest men I had known in all my twenty years, and in fact, few have surpassed that in the decades since he was my teacher. He's the reason I signed up for his seminar on Thomas Merton, a thinker I knew nothing about. I see how, according to the typewriter-font syllabus that flies out of my ivory pages of Merton's autobiography, *The Seven Storey Mountain*, I must have given some sort of presentation to the class on *Conjectures of a Guilty Bystander* in the fall of 1981. What did I understand of Merton's epiphany in 1958, his mystical awakening in Louisville, Kentucky, on the corner of Fourth and Walnut? I have no idea what I conveyed to my six classmates about the core of one of his most famous essays. I only know that now, at the age of sixty, I find its message deeply, reassuringly beautiful. Maybe I did then, too.

The passage is one of his most quoted—it pops up all over the internet. In it, he captures his momentous experience of being flooded with love on a city street, just an ordinary day. He's overcome with how it shines from every angle: his own love toward all people, God's celebratory love of us, the light connecting each and every one of us to each other, the beauty our hearts all hold. It was a life-changing—a faith-changing—realization for him. In the heart of Louisville, now, there's a copper plaque on that exact spot to venerate it. Titled "A Revelation" it stands near the street sign that reads "W. Muhammad Ali Blvd./Thomas Merton Square".

What reached me at that time was a bizarre coincidence during my classmate Jeff's presentation. Jeff was a very talented photographer and had done a slideshow taking photos that represented Merton's ideas from *Asian Journal*. Jeff also did art installations with objects, and for some reason, he'd brought in an old, rickety electric fan on a metal pole to blow on us as he presented. His work was always stellar, and as he closed up, there was a silence. George had a strange expression in his blue eyes, his gray hair blowing. We waited.

"What is it?" we asked.

He pointed to the fan and nodded.

We still didn't understand. Suddenly the fan began to tip over. Jeff lunged too late to grab the stand. The whole thing crashed loudly onto the floor.

"I'm so sorry, George!" Jeff knelt to pick up the pieces.

"You don't know, do you?" George looked at each of us.

"Know what?" Leela asked.

"How Merton died."

We'd only read his work; we hadn't gotten that far.

George said, "Merton was electrocuted in the bath by a fan. In Thailand. That's how he died. I thought that's why you brought in the fan."

"No," Jeff blinked, shocked. "I just—saw it at the Common's thrift store and on a whim, just thought I would—include it—"

It was a spooky seminar. Certainly, it had a Ouija-board weirdness, a strange séance vibe. That doesn't interest me—it might have when I was younger—but not anymore. What I understand is that in my study of Merton, maybe I did things in reverse. I crossed paths with Merton's nightmarish death first, then I could spend the ensuing decades focusing on how he strived so valiantly to see clearly, under his feet, the path of God's will for his life.

It shouldn't have surprised me that, as I dove into my research of the psalms, he would meet me there, perfect as a pair of mallards floating down the river.

One of Connecticut's biggest collections of books on the world's religions is housed at the University of St. Joseph, founded by the Sisters of Mercy. The librarian limped with her cane to take me to the shelves I needed. As we disappeared into shadowy stacks, the scent of old paper pulp intoxicated me with a feeling of *home*. Libraries have always been home for me. The current world of Wikipedia and Google has changed so much since the days of gathering info using card catalogs and the Dewey Decimal. We wended our way to the aisle, and she turned on the light to the collection of a hundred old psalm books, then left me to the task of standing with my head bent to read, and reach, for the spines. The covers were all the same faded color, as if, instead of light, the years of untouched dust had sun-bleached them all matching cornflower blue.

I became overwhelmed and despondent. Why should I write yet another book on the psalms, when there were already so many? When I didn't know how to really approach them? My eyes glazed over all the titles. And then, sticking up, oversized and seagull-gray, I read "*Bread in the Wilderness*: Merton" and I laughed because I never knew he wrote on the psalms, but of course he did. Merton wrote on *everything*. I slid the book out and sat silently in a study carrel for hours reading it. Most of it was over my head. I was used to that with Merton. But I also knew that certain lines would break through. Something gorgeous. Like this, from the chapter "Poetry, Symbolism, and Typology":

> That too is why an age, like the one we live in, in which cosmic symbolism has been almost forgotten and submerged under a tidal wave of trademarks, political party buttons, advertising and propaganda slogans and all the rest—is necessarily an age of mass psychosis. A world in which the poet can find practically no material in the common substance of everyday life, in which he is driven crazy in his search for the vital symbols that have been buried alive under a mountain of cultural garbage, can only end up, like ours, in self-destruction.[1]

I flip to the front of the book: Merton wrote this in 1953. Even in just those few lines, it's easy to see why his readers stick with him; he reaches beyond the cacophony of the twentieth century straight into the atonal twenty-first.

And then I land on the exact sentence that I need to continue on my own path. "It is useless, then, to seek some secret esoteric 'method' of reciting the Psalter in order to 'get contemplation.'"[2] I understand what he's offering. I don't have to complicate the psalms. I can let them be. I can keep doing what I've done, which is, quite simply, *read them*. And reflect. There is no secret way that eludes me. There is only my way, and I have the same desire he did: to allow God to find me.

A fact comes to me that blows me away and yet makes so much sense in understanding the architecture of his faith. As a Trappist monk, when Merton was at the hermitage of the Abbey of Our Lady of Gethsemane in Kentucky, he sang the psalms with his brotherhood five times a day. It is their distinct way of climbing, their devotion. And silence the rest of the time. This means that he went through — singing — the entire round of 150 psalms *every two weeks*. It's beyond my comprehension, and yet I would love to try this.

What would happen to me if I really *poured it on*? I'm curious. I have found a Trappist monastery — based on the format of Merton's hermitage — in New York State, and I could drive there. On their website it reads, that since they follow the rules of St. Benedict, "All guests who present themselves are to be welcomed as Christ." It's intimidating. Could I withstand that much acceptance from a stranger? Could I embody the Rumi line, "Today I recognize that I am the guest the mystics talk about"?

Being welcomed like that. I want to dare myself to feel this. Maybe one day I will ring the bell at that abbey and listen for the opening of the door. What would it be like to see the look on their faces when they treat me like Christ, but instead of him, it's me?

+ + +

I find a Richard Rohr quote about Merton that fills me with a sense of indebtedness and gratitude. He writes, "I believe that he almost single handedly pulled back the veil and helped us see that we all had lost the older tradition of contemplation, the older methods for quieting the mind and heart and seeing 'spiritual things spiritually' (1 Cor. 2:13) had been lost."[3]

If I understand it, Rohr is basically saying that Merton changed the face of Catholicism so thoroughly that I can actually identify Merton's reach in my daily life: I have spent years now trying to quiet my mind. I often think of who Merton was as a small child, and the abyss he faced at the devastating death of his Quaker mother when he was six. This motherless child grew up to be a man who never stopped hungering for, and often finding, bread in the wilderness. This loss created one of the most extraordinary seekers of our times.

+ + +

Last year when the traveling exhibit of Merton's photographs came to the art gallery of Wisdom House, a spiritual retreat center in the hills west of me, my connection to Merton took a permanent turn toward understanding. By seeing where his eye was drawn, I felt I was meeting him face-to-face. Thirty-five of his black-and-white photos were displayed with the theme "A Hidden Wholeness: The Zen Photography of Thomas Merton." The photos were technically near-perfect, their titles simple:

Solitary Chair
Open Barn Door
Bare Branch
Window

His art was all about looking directly at what is right there, in light, and not just seeing the shadow, but honoring it. What impacted me was the way, without words, he articulated his vision. In most of what he writes, he leaves me in the dust, but his photos? I could grasp them.

To see the world, close-up, exactly as he saw it. To see what he thought was worthy as I walked around and around that room (grateful to have the solitude) and letting his images soak into me. His art was sublime; I peered clearly inside him. All the years I've witnessed my students calling forth the fragments, writing lyrics, poems and stories, setting themselves free, free from within—it's how I've gotten to know them, and it's how I've loved them. This is what art does.

Now, a framed pumice-colored wheelbarrow leans against a white barn, wooden handles straight up with parallel smoky shadows on the wall. Behind foggy weeds, the barest whisper of a wooden crucifix shape in the reinforcement of the barn door. Finding this shape in the ordinary day. The subtlety of it and the strangely nourishing truth of it tilting there. Nothing forced, no strain. Effortless cropped beauty as you walk. The work resonated with the ideas of the great Irish writer John O'Donohue, "May you take time to celebrate the quiet miracles that need no attention."

I am led right back to the psalms. Merton's photos are all about how light touches our world. Like my friend Patrice the painter says, "The lightest light touches the darkest dark." It's about accepting all of it. The entire range. All the overlap and all the edges. What if we just come home to how ordinary things hold our sacredness? My favorite Merton photograph is a close-range image of a tire tread left in fresh snow. I love that he lowered himself, perhaps kneeling, to get close to the pattern of it. And maybe what I really love is how the image is of a car, a road; it leads to his most famous prayer of traveling:

> My Lord God, I have no idea where I am going. I do not see the road ahead of me. I cannot know for certain where it will end. Nor do I really know myself, and the fact that I think I am following Your will does not mean that I am actually doing so. But I believe that the desire to please You does in fact please You. And I hope I have that desire in all that I am doing. I hope that I will never do anything apart from that desire. And I know that, if I do this, You will lead me by the right road, though I may know nothing about it. Therefore I will trust You always

though I may seem to be lost and in the shadow of death. I will not fear, for You are ever with me, and You will never leave me to face my perils alone. Amen.[4]

David

Dancer

The first time I traveled to Italy in 2014, I had no idea that Michelangelo's infamous *David* was a sculpture honoring the person who wrote seventy-three of the 150 psalms (and set the tone for them all). I had never made that connection. Standing in the Florence piazza in front of the towering figure as it dazzled in the afternoon April sun, my mouth agape at how any human being could shape such a thing out of marble, I didn't even notice the slingshot slung over his left shoulder to kill Goliath; I only registered that recently. So though I've leaned into his words for years, my deepening understanding of King David the man, the actual writer, has been slow and started out extremely rudimentary. Now that I'm eagerly finding out about him, it's daunting to try and pin him down. In fact, he cannot be pinned down. A magnificent warrior and king, and also a man who made immoral decisions, his legacy and his poetry infiltrates the world today.

As I began my psalms research with C.S. Lewis, one of the first stories to grab my attention was a passage about how David "danced with such abandon that one of his wives…thought he was making a fool of himself," but he "didn't care" because he was "rejoicing in the Lord."[5] This was an electrifying image. Within a few days, I came across the exact passage in Samuel 6. There are times reading the Old Testament where page after page of dense text eludes me, and then suddenly it all comes into crisp, sharp focus. This is such a passage. I don't know what a "linen ephod" is, but I can guess. David dances "without restraint" in it and there's "shouting and blowing of trumpets" (6:15). One of his wives looks down and he's "leaping and capering" and for this, she "despises him in her heart." (When I told my friend Lola this story we laughed when she said, "Wow, nothing changes!").

My whole life I've loved watching men dance. My earliest crush was on Gene Kelly as he grinned with delight under his dripping fedora, full of love to the point of overflowing in "Singing in the Rain." As his song expands, he takes up more and more space on the cobblestones around the lamppost, getting wider and wilder in his splashing. I'm a diehard Mick Jagger fan, and I recall the words of C.C., one of my best friends who is like a sister, when I took her to see the Rolling Stones at a stadium (filled with shouting, and instead of lyres and trumpets, the bass and electric guitars), and she first laid eyes on him and wondered, "He's so emotionally open when he moves." Mick Jagger stomps across the stage, pigeon-toed and goofy, exuberant, twitchy, not athletic but boyishly lithe. Men dancing: pop culture bursts with them. Prince scissoring his legs in velvet high heels. A young Elvis? Explosive moves, both spontaneous and symmetrical, he found freedom within patterns. James Brown flying high and alighting not on his feet but satin legs wide in a split. Patrick Swayze, in the finale of *Dirty Dancing* as he strut-walks right at us, so cool, returning to lift Baby high; her arms swan-wide, he holds her aloft in fuchsia lights and applause.

These stars cavort for the high and joy of it, they're thrilling to watch—and it can be argued they're jolted with a holy spirit. But

David wasn't just dancing, he was a king letting loose on the dance floor for *God*. Here he was, having survived bloody battles, vile hatred, beheading a giant, all the details we know of his life, and he was unashamed to publicly express his love. Not romantic love of a woman, or celebrating a newly married couple, but being unabashedly vulnerable in showing his devotion. I've never actually seen a man dance for God. It's extraordinary to think about. And when I do ponder it, I think, that as a musician, he must have had a strong sense of rhythm and movement, and combined with his strength and good looks, it must have been quite a sight. Yet his wife was ashamed of him and called him an "empty-headed fool."

Here was a man who placed his connection to God at the forefront of his life, dancing, ecstatic, in front of the crowds of people he ruled. Ever since this image has come to me, in the last few days, I can't stop thinking about it. It intrudes, like the memory of a concert, on my most ordinary tasks. Even now, going downstairs to stir the yellow lentil stew on this Saturday, as I descend the stairs in my slippers, I feel David, leaping and twisting, and I wonder: If I just let go of my anxieties and fears, could I come closer God, not primarily due to my litany of sorrows, but through an unsung joy? Isn't this what the psalms offer, ultimately—the chance to both lament *and* praise?

David wrote, "My heart leaps for joy, and I praise him with my whole body" (Ps 28:8).

How breathtaking that this poet explores the arc of human emotion in the way that he does. To be fully *alive* is to fully *feel*. When people talk of a romantic relationship, they say how in order for the relationship to thrive you have to bring "all of yourself" to the other. David models how this is true in our relationship to God. Like a lover, he holds nothing back, keeps no secrets. In all the psalms, page after page, the speaker is taking the time to talk, to share, to prioritize, to connect. To build a bridge to God where truth can flow across it, and love can travel both ways.

Dave

I'm going to leave that *Dave* typo because it's fairly ridiculous to think of King David as Dave, and perhaps irreverent; still, it's another way to approach this work with less intimidation. I made myself laugh when I read that mistake, and since much of my exploration has been serious, I welcome a moment of levity. He, of all people, knew the rock-bottom emotions of the destruction he left in his wake, the grotesque way his own life was misshapen by his mistakes, his lust, and his rage. Both a deeply flawed human and magnificent artist, we can call him Dave to honor that he was both kind and human. People in recovery from addictions sometimes say, to quell their pride and find a commonality with ordinary routines in the day-to-day world, "You're just another Bozo on the bus." People also often take issue with this phrase, as it is a bit negative, and flippant. But the point is taken. No one is so special that their path takes them beyond the routes where the bus of life takes everyone, where everyone, riding on the planet *together*, goes.

Father

According to biblical history, David wrote Psalm 34 about the time he pretended to be stark raving crazy, "feigning madness" in order to be set free of the danger of being murdered in 1 Samuel 21. The visuals of this story are incredibly alluring, including drooling in his beard. David's entire *life* was overloaded with cinematic possibilities. With this psalm in particular, I'm drawn to the depth of his thanksgiving, as he's grateful for God being there when he sunk down into the sorrow of his heart: "The Lord is close to the brokenhearted and saves those whose spirit is crushed" (Ps 34:19).

We hear about a spirit being broken, but it's more agonizing to have it *crushed*. Crushed underneath the tonnage of a tumultuous event, or a series of them, as many lives are, including David's. It's one thing to withstand this ourselves, but it's the hardest watching the suffering of those we love. If we believe that God is with our loved ones—not just *with* them but even better, *close* to them—can we take deeper breaths through it all?

Our children will suffer, but can we trust that God is there? In the language of Twelve-Step recovery, this might be expressed as "she has her own Higher Power." This is often said to try to comfort parents when they realize their sheer, utter powerlessness over a terrifying addiction one of their children might be lost within. It can apply to cancer, racial evils, break-ups, betrayals, sexual violence, bullying, failure—the list overflows. No matter how much you love your child, you'll come to a crossroads where you realize that your love can't block the blows falling upon them. David lived this. When his son was sick, he lay on the ground pleading with God for seven days. But his child died. So yes, this father knew *crushed*.

I've written about my love of Mary as a mother, the way I wonder how she endured watching her son's body and spirit expire. She's gotten me through the hardest times witnessing children—my own children and my students—suffer. If I trust that something loving and holy is close to them, then what? I know they aren't walking through the valley of death all alone. I can envision my loved ones headed toward the tranquility of Psalm 23. I pray that God is close to them throughout every long, excruciating night, for every item currently being added to the list.

Broken Hallelujah

There's much contemporary, stronger language I could use here to describe him, profanity even, a synonym for *screw up*. David made both heroic and horrible decisions. "Flawed human" might be a bit mild a description for a man who slept with the stunning Bathsheba after he spied her on a rooftop, got her pregnant, had her husband killed, then married her. The son that came from this transgression is one that David lost. He was beside himself with grief, shame, remorse, and self-loathing.

The most unequaled artist's reflections on this part of his life is Leonard Cohen's "Hallelujah." Few people realize that this is the story of David and Bathsheba. I'm not sure how that song fits into the children's animation film *Shrek*, but it does. The song is everywhere, and rightly so. There's such *soul* in the piece. Many, many artists have covered this song but I believe the most sublime version is done by k.d. lang.

This flawed human asks for forgiveness for his "broken hallelujah." David, in Psalm 51, asks to be fully, wholly, forever forgiven. What has touched me in my study of him is that somewhere inside, in his center, lay his hidden treasure, the one Jesus would come to speak of: "For where your treasure is, there also will your heart be" (Matthew 6:21). An ability to know that he was *worthy* of love and forgiveness, and that God *would* forgive him for the colossal mess he made. Can we hurt others deeply and still be forgiven? David somehow knew the answer was yes. He could. In my understanding of the family lineage, this is part of the reason why David foreshadows the possibility that a messiah, a savior, a Christ—will come. As I reread this psalm, the title says, *The Miserere*. I finally look up this word. It means "mercy." Of course. My understanding of that word keeps deepening. The Renaissance composer Gregoria Allegri wrote a choral piece for this psalm. You may have heard it somberly performed during Holy Week.

Psalm 51

For the leader. A psalm of David, when Nathan the prophet came to him after he had gone in to Bathsheba.

I

Have mercy on me, God, in accord with your merciful love;
   in your abundant compassion blot out my transgressions.
Thoroughly wash away my guilt;
   and from my sin cleanse me.
For I know my transgressions;
   my sin is always before me.
Against you, you alone have I sinned;
   I have done what is evil in your eyes
So that you are just in your word,
   and without reproach in your judgment.
Behold, I was born in guilt,
   in sin my mother conceived me.
Behold, you desire true sincerity;
   and secretly you teach me wisdom.
Cleanse me with hyssop,* that I may be pure;
   wash me, and I will be whiter than snow.
You will let me hear gladness and joy;
   the bones you have crushed will rejoice.

II

Turn away your face from my sins;
   blot out all my iniquities.
A clean heart create for me, God;
   renew within me a steadfast spirit.
Do not drive me from before your face,
   nor take from me your holy spirit.

Warrior

In my desire to underscore his role as a warrior, I planned on pointing
out four consecutive psalms that chronicle David's calling out to God

in the midst of the relentless inhumanity he faced. I'd been struck repeatedly by how contemporary Psalms 140, 141, 142, and 143 were, and I thought it'd be useful for trying to get a foothold in the violence of our times, helping us articulate the confused anguish we hold within.

But when I went back to the poems, something new became crystalline. I wanted to isolate those linked messages of crying out to God, but now it doesn't seem like an accurate interpretation to compartmentalize them. Psalm 138—*Hymn of a Grateful Heart*—and then my beloved Psalm 139, about God's omnipresence and omniscience, are placed right before the sequence. Psalm 144 and 145 follow with lines such as "Your reign is a reign for all ages."

The psalms keep teaching me that to be emotionally and spiritually whole, there's no drawing lines inside the human heart. It's like my students keep showing me. We can feel it all. Rejected and radiant. I think the psalms show our inner lives are a celestial place, a Milky Way, and as John Muir wrote about everything being connected, "When we try to pick out anything by itself, we find it hitched to everything else in the Universe."

King David

Whoever he was as a warrior, as a king, as a compass pointing that Christ was on his way, I deeply appreciate all that. I cannot help it that I admire him most as a *poet*. Day by day, my reverence has grown. It's really that simple. My professional specialty is twentieth-century American literature, and I love so many writers (ask my students, who always tease me that I say they are all "my favorite"). Though writing in an ancient time, David is no different to me. However, because his work is entwined with the longing for God, I have the highest place in my heart for him. I feel this way about the thirteenth-century poet Hafiz, too.

If you are wondering how to know which psalms David wrote, many translations will say it at the beginning of the psalm. No scholar really knows how many people wrote the psalms, and maybe even the ones attributed to David are by someone else. All I know is that the Psalter is crammed with words that made me underline sentences I yearn to return to, and so I write "beauty" in the margins.

There is really no end to these poems. Is there any "finishing" Michelangelo's *David*? Of course not, and wonderfully so. I'd like to let David's rendering of spring have the last word now. Psalm 65 sings of a lush, unbroken, detailed description of spring in the desert. The stakes are very high, as in this geographical setting, rain isn't something to detest and complain about but to celebrate its "visit" (65:10). Rain means food, flowers, relief, flocks. Everything connected by alliteration.

Where I live, rain isn't always welcomed, but in David's reality it was a blessing, worth six long lines of poetry, capturing the earth as it is softening. *How* is he doing this? I'm stumped. He's pinpointing the transition that has happened as it is *still* happening, alive and moving, yet he frames it while it's thrumming. It's not hyperbole to say: I'm in awe of how he writes of awe.

Distant peoples stand in awe of your marvels;
   the places of morning and evening you make resound with joy.
You visit the earth and water it,
   make it abundantly fertile.
God's stream is filled with water;
   you supply their grain.
Thus do you prepare it:
   you drench its plowed furrows,
   and level its ridges.
With showers you keep it soft,
   blessing its young sprouts.

You adorn the year with your bounty;
    your paths drip with fruitful rain.
The meadows of the wilderness also drip;
    the hills are robed with joy.
The pastures are clothed with flocks,
    the valleys blanketed with grain;
    they cheer and sing for joy.

What to Call You When I Call Out to You

I don't call God what the psalms call God: *Lord*. I never use this word, except when it's spoken as part of Mass, and in reading the poems. As a writer, it's always confounded me to talk about spirituality. How do we define our terms so we know if we're talking about the same thing? In recovery, the more neutral "Higher Power" serves millions of people asking for help to be set free of addictions to vodka, Oxy, casinos, as they commit to establishing a connection with something beyond themselves. I find the Jewish use of "G-d" to make a great deal of sense; it honors the fact that alphabets cannot capture something so vast. In my work at Light on the Hill, "The Divine" slowly became part of my vocabulary, like a windswept erosion revealing the words, clearly carved. After reading Hafiz for many years, I've also come to think of God as "The Beloved": so my own vocabulary keeps evolving. I remember when my spiritual director Alice, shaped by her years of studying Sufism, the mystical aspect of Islam, said, "There's something different about saying the word *Allah. Ahhh-laaa*. It's more open, and resonates differently than *God*."

I love the musical sensitivity of this.

When the Catholic Church switched from "Holy Ghost" to "Holy Spirit," it changed everything for me as a kid, because, quite frankly, I took things very literally and watched a lot of *Scooby Doo* with various ethereal creatures; "spirit" sets me free.

I'll be candid here, though I hesitate to share this, fearing judgment. But I carry an interior barrier in using "God the Father." I could write raw pages about why the word *father* was never a bridge toward the holy for me. But in another language, I might begin to open to it; when I went to Cortona's Palm Sunday Mass and I heard, in Italian, *Padre Nostro* instead of *Our Father*, I loved that.

I'm equally intrigued by the first chapter of the *Tao De Ching*, and the Taoist notion of the *Ten Thousand Things*:

> *The word that can be spoken is not the eternal Word.*
> *Unnamed, It is the source of heaven and earth.*
> *Named, It is the Mother of all things.*[6]

Whatever words we use I believe we're all described in the first lines of Psalms 42, "As the deer longs for stream of water, so my soul longs for you, O God." and I believe this longing unites us.

I want to close with names I love the *most*, titles of the Blessed Virgin Mary:

> Morning Star,
> Cause of Our Joy,
> Dwelling Place for God,
> Lily Among Thorns,
> Star of the Sea,
> Our Lady of Guadalupe,
> Rose Ever Blooming.

And my own callings, the ones I've made to and for her:

> My Mother, All Day and All Night,
> Dawn of Half-Remembered Dreams,

Protector of the Highway,
Protector of My Heart,
Protector of the Tiny.

Urbi et Orbi

I kept this a secret for decades until recently: I had a mystical vision when I was ten years old. It's my most precious childhood memory, and I've learned, now that I'm sharing more of my inner life, that others also have treasured memories connected to "Let It Be." My mother, young and beautiful in our kitchen, stood at the sink in her bathrobe dotted with forget-me-nots. She was, like always, in profile, staring out the window, lost in her thoughts, watching the birds at her feeder. I nibbled a warm, gooey cinnamon Pop-Tart. We lived outside Philadelphia in a town called Blue Bell, but my mother tuned the clock radio to WABC from New York City, and the new Beatles hit began. Hearing Paul McCartney sing about "Mother Mary" coming to him in times of trouble, I suddenly felt Mary's presence flooding the kitchen with my mother and I, an extraordinary peace like sunlight bathing me. The Blessed Mother glowed near the pantry, with love.

Now I tune my old boom box radio to WJMJ with the tagline "Catholic radio, where faith meets life." I've always found this station comforting because it plays the songs from the seventies. Neil Diamond, Tony Orlando and Dawn, songs like "Let It Be." Oddly, WJMJ, when they run the news at the top of each hour, uses the news from WABC, just like the news my mother listened to in that long ago kitchen. I keep my radio on 24/7 near the toaster; music on the counter makes me feel like where I live is really *home*.

Now, isolated in the pandemic, it's nerve-wracking when these hourly news reports come on with coronavirus updates of infections and deaths. There are still soothing Jim Croce oldies and the interludes with Father John, a priest whose online temperament is appealingly sincere, and who offers inspiring, well-articulated messages that still, even in a pandemic, redirect my fears toward hope. The Hail Marys help me to remember I'm not alone as I empty the dishwasher. At 7:00 p.m. the nightly show called *Afterglow* includes affirmations and Ave Marias to help you reflect on your day. The last thing I do at night in my pajamas is darken the house, leaving only the outdoor porch light on, and one overhead stove light, and then I lower the volume on the radio for the nightly classical music, hours of faint kitchen-violins.

But last night at 7:00, as I was upstairs writing, I heard a man speaking. It wasn't Father John, but a vulnerable, unfamiliar voice, bare, and completely stripped. I froze, listening. Who was this? I quietly padded down the stairs to get closer. I remembered that I'd read Pope Francis was going to speak at 1:00, in Rome. I knew that here in America, we are six hours ahead, and realized this was his special message. A woman translated. He spoke slowly in the lyrical cadence of Italian, and then we heard the same words, in the voice of a woman, in English.

I'd never heard this pope give any sort of homily. I was entranced. My weeks off from school as the pandemic spread have been terrifying. His country, with thousands of caskets, already had been hit by the virus so hard. He spoke of storms, about not just believing in Jesus, but trusting him—always my biggest challenge, moving from faith to trust. I couldn't help but have my "writer's ear" tuned to how the writing flowed, the images within. I know good writing when I hear it, because I can feel it. And this was gorgeous prose. The pope said we need to invite Jesus into our boat, and he sustained that image throughout.

His words pulsed. *"Ci siamo resi conto che siamo sulla stessa barca, tutti fragili e disorientati…tutti noi abbiamo chiamato ora insieme."* And then the American translator, a woman with emotion in her voice. "We have realized that we are on the same boat, all of us fragile and disoriented… all of us called now together." The words came in two languages, spoken by both male and female, like a mother and father, a sister and brother, a son and daughter. I stood in the afterglow, transfixed. Having spent the weeks fitful and twitchy, I waited to lose interest. But his words kept unfurling, and somehow, miraculously, while isolated in my house, I was included in his vision from across the ocean. *"Quanti insegnanti:* How many teachers?" he asked. I was valued.

And so this morning I looked it up, and learned the speech he gave is traditionally and liturgically only given at Christmas and Easter. It's called *Urbi et Orbi.*

But these are uncharted times. *Urbi et Orbi.* To the city and to the world.

He spoke to an empty city. To a terrified world. As a member of a Franciscan church, I respected him years ago for choosing his name and bringing Francis more fully into the twenty-first century, but I had no set opinion on him. Now, I admire this man who, during a plague, takes a metaphor and lets it flow. In the global shuttering he has given us anchors and rudders and hope. When I find a video recording of this message, before beginning, he steps somberly through a lonely square. Rain falls upon Rome. The camera pans to a crucifix, and focuses close up on a wet nail hammered through Christ's palm as a flying creature still lifts its wings, and in the ache of the world's silence, the call of a gull breaks through.

Refuge

I wake up to begin writing, and in the dim winter light, I see where my eye is drawn when I open my broken Bible to the psalms. *Refuge* appears, over and over. What exactly is refuge? It's vastly different than shelter. Refuge is deeper, scarier. The stakes are higher when you need refuge. *Shelter* is from temperatures dropping and the chance of rain. You can probably make it through without shelter. But without refuge, you're vulnerable and truly alone. Refuge is wind blowing the cedars as far as they will bend, thunder that jolts you and an absolutely black night that has suddenly fallen. And you're running toward home. The need for it is deeper in the body. When you find shelter, you can calmly peer out. But the need for refuge makes you look within.

I could never add up the number of hours I've spent alone staring out the window at that void. Those are the deepest darkest loneliest hours. I feel that darkness filling me, as I am part of it. *In you, Lord, I take refuge; let me never be put to shame* (Ps 31:1). When I remember to say a prayer, it comes as a cluster of stars on the periphery, and I'm not quite sure I even saw any green sparkle, but I try again. A Hail Mary. A *Jesus Please*. I can't even call that relief "embers" because embers stay awhile.

When I cannot sleep because I am reliving some conflict I endured that day, one I feel I cannot undo, when I'm imagining some future event which I fear is going to flood me with more heartache and sink me, and God, at last, finds me in the dark, I fall asleep, and when I wake up, I don't know at what point I finally let that refuge enclose me.

The psalms are all about the contrasts in our lives. Like a riveting black-and-white photo, there's gradations: vivid cool to dramatic warm to dramatic cool. Refuge honors the challenge of the silver tone moments turning to noir.

Steadfast

I suddenly understood a word. By "understanding," I mean I felt it, not as an idea, a thought, but as something anchored within me. The setting is embarrassingly unglamorous. I walked in the overhead spotlights behind the Big Y grocery store, headed home through the back parking lot where the eighteen-wheelers idle, ten o'clock on a Sunday night, preparing for the beginning of my workweek holding a paper bag. In it, I had the plain foods of my simple life. Frozen green beans, a pint of fresh raspberries, a can of Goya kidney beans, and two small Greek yogurts. Breakfast for Monday and Tuesday. I'd add the other ingredients to items from my pantry to make a crockpot of minestrone soup, enough to last me a few days. I thought perhaps this was a version of the Zen saying "Chop wood and carry water" to describe embracing the beauty of the mundane.

I felt inexplicably satisfied realizing I was completely provided for in the night. I held everything I needed and even with my compromised left hand, I had enough strength to carry it. *Steadfast love* came floating up from my heart. I knew it was something more dependable, longer-lasting, than gratitude. And it wasn't quite *praise*.

The best part of that moment was that I didn't feel elated by it. I recognized that it was beyond a "good feeling"—it was faith. It was steady; it was steadfast. Such a perfect word, the beauty of the "st" at the start of the word, and the end. Like bookends holding up the middle assortment of vowels. Holding me up too.

The translation is also lovely.

Steadfast from *hesed, hhesed*, concrete meaning "to bow, like a stork, head bent down."

I never hear this word in conversation. In fact, I don't find it anywhere but the psalms, where *steadfast love* appears 127 times. God's love is steadfast. I do think that God's love for me is reliable, constant, unwavering. As I left the intense globe of the parking lot light and entered the sudden dark path, I thought, once again, though I know my *faith* is always fairly strong, my *trust* in God is not.

Mercy

Mercy died at 3 a.m.

Mercy, my friend Rafael's mother, had lived in a nursing home for several years with severe Alzheimer's. Every day at five o'clock Rafael pulled the little chain on his Emeralite Bankers lamp, officially ending his day as the creative writing department chair at my school. He drove a few towns over to spoon-feed Mercy her supper because, alongside losing her ability to speak in both her native Spanish and acquired English, "Ta" (short for *Abuelita*) could no longer feed herself. As arts teachers, we've worked alongside each other for years. We're very close. Rafael often texted us photos of her round face, beaming. Often she was holding her little doll named Lonnie. In this way, we all shared in Mercy's magic.

I cannot think of any son who loved his mother as fully as Rafael loved Mercy.

At the end, because of coronavirus, he could no longer be near her to feed her. He had one final "window visit" with her, separated by glass. Then the virus took her. And now, I don't send flowers, because I am not even sure if people want to receive them in this time of bleaching everything that crosses our thresholds. I want to send him daffodils, so instead of real live cooling blossoms, I send him a Georgia O'Keeffe postcard, one of my favorites, perfect flowing opening yellows. A bit off center in the painting two flowers are together, almost creating an infinity symbol in the way their shapes overlap.

How do we find mercy? We become, as St. Teresa of Avila said, the hands of Christ, because "he has no hands on earth other than ours." So we hold spoons for others and feed them. We buy armloads of daffodils, like a woman I read about this morning, a woman in New Jersey who works in the morgue. Who each day fills her arms with yellow bouquets and when she enters the refrigerated trucks stacked with the dead, almost all of whom died alone, she places a single daffodil upon each and every body bag.[7] A short poem by Wordsworth comes to me.

I wandered lonely as a cloud
That floats on high o'er vales and hills,
When all at once I saw a crowd,
A host, of golden daffodils.

Whatever "mercy" is, an understanding of it has eluded me. Not because I haven't tried. On my dashboard I've tucked a tattered prayer card of the Divine Mercy with the rays of light pouring from Jesus's heart. For 80,000 miles, everywhere I've driven, its gone before me, and still, mercy remains unclear. In my prayer area I keep a little prayer book with a litany of praises from Saint Faustina, the nun who received all the Divine Mercy messages. *Divine Mercy, in which we are all immersed, I trust in You.* I couldn't remember the name of the retreat house where I got it, over a decade ago, until just now, and I laughed: it's from Mercy by the Sea in Madison, Connecticut.

I'm at the very beginning of understanding mercy, and perhaps Mercy's death is bringing me closer to, if not quite grasping it, at least touching it. But this is backwards, because I think it's not about me chasing after mercy, but seeing how it's already here. When Rafael wrote to me about the death of his mom, he said, "I've never been without Mercy (and I'm still not)." Mercy's obituary reads, "In lieu of flowers, please read the poem 'in time's a noble mercy of proportion' by e.e. cummings and love one another in Mercy's memory." In honor of this loving mother, I look the poem up:

> in time's a noble mercy of proportion
> with generosities beyond believing

Something has shifted, and I see how goodness and mercy link. Maybe I don't have to make it so hard. Maybe it's as simple — and I use this example from my meditation down by the pond yesterday — as calling a Red-Wing Blackbird a Red-Wing Blackbird because it's a black bird with red wings. Goodness and mercy. Maybe it's right here, the Mercy with a capital M and the mercy right before our eyes, lowercase.

> The moon and stars to rule the night,
>   for his mercy endures forever. (Ps 136:9)

Two Dusks

I had committed to reading the psalms every day for not quite two years when I had one of the most explosive verbal fights I've ever had with anyone. Except this one wasn't even with a person, but with God, and I finally understood the rock-bottom despair of the psalms of lament.

A January blizzard had dumped two feet of snow in the Northeast, I was halfway to the retreat center in upstate New York where I'd been studying (also for the last two years), and the highways were a mess. My windshield wiper fluid wasn't spraying out, and every time a bullying truck driver overtook me on Route 84 West, my windshield became a smear of salt and sand and I could not see. I pulled into the Stormville Rest Stop, cars spinning in the slush. I snatched a handful of loose snow from along the sidewalk and tossed it on my windshield to clear it.

My phone rang. "Hey!" C.C. greeted me. "How are you, girl?"

"I've got a few hours to go. Headed to Light on the Hill."

"I thought this was one of your weekends. How're you holding up?"

I always tell her the truth. "I'm a mess. I close on the house Monday. Then Wednesday, I get divorced."

"Wow."

"I know, right? Our home for eighteen years. A twenty-five-year marriage. In a forty-eight hour span, bam! All of it's going to be gone."

In the bitter cold I could barely grasp my phone. Trucks flew past on the highway as I strained to hear her.

"Just remember," C.C. cautioned, "that when you actually get divorced, there might be a new layer of grief."

This scared me—C.C. was a gifted therapist and always had uncanny insights. I stared out at the blue-white fields and the sky, all peachy-rose tints. My family of four had been blown apart. "But it can't hurt any more than it already does, could it?"

She considered this. "I don't know. I hope not. I gotta go. I'm outside the girls' school to pick them up. Have a good weekend. I love you."

"Love you too."

I steered through the wet snow and gunned it back into the traffic. Cut off from C.C., I began to plummet. *What's the point of all this?* I was midway through the three-year commitment of Finding Your Hidden Treasure. This was the second winter of bracing slick weather conditions. I loved the course and the intimacy of the group. My new friends, most of whom lived close to the retreat center, admired my commitment to growing. I was almost always the first one at the Inner Light Lodge; my classmates had come to expect it.

As I drove, I didn't feel connected to any of them. "Oh my God," I shrieked as another truck left my windshield tan and opaque. I was going 75 miles an hour peering through a hole the size of a mitten. Both outside mirrors were completely crusted with sand. I cursed the world. "*Screw this!*" I took the next exit, following an arrow to the Mobil station. My soon-to-be ex-husband had taken care of my car for twenty-five years. I never paid a dime for a mechanic; I had no idea where the windshield wiper fluid even went. How was I supposed to learn how to do all this now?

I belted my coat tight and headed into the mini-mart. A young man with his back to me was stocking cigarettes, "Do you have windshield wiper fluid?"

As he turned, I was taken aback by his T-shirt. His entire torso was covered with Our Lady of Guadalupe. The Blessed Mother's blue robe and spiked yellow rays glowed from within his unzipped hoodie. "Yes, sure." He pointed to the rack of plastic bottles filled with aquamarine liquid.

"Thank you." I handed him my debit card and sheepishly asked, "Do you know where the fluid goes?"

His smile revealed eyeteeth high on his gums. "Don't feel bad. My mom doesn't know either. Give me a moment. Pull your car over there."

Outside, I stamped my boots to keep warm. With the hood popped open, he poured the fluid in. Grateful for his kindness, I squelched my urge to begin confessing the litany of my last three years of heartache to the kid. *My husband had a heart attack, then six weeks later I was diagnosed with cancer, then his best friend died—then I fell and shattered—then we—.*

When he slammed the hood, I fished out a ten-dollar bill. "Here, please take this, and thank you."

"No, ma'am, it's okay."

I got into the car and flipped on the wipers. Watery teal blue sprayed up, soaking the sand, and the windshield became flawlessly clear. He gave me a thumbs up sign and loped back inside. All was well, my crisis over. I returned to Route 84, then began the leg of the trip on 17 West. I got sandwiched in the middle lane between two eighteen-wheelers, and as they muscled by me the ice, sand, and salt spit and sprayed off their mud flaps coating my windshield, making it opaque again. When I flicked on the wipers and slammed the fluid release with my hand, nothing squirted. The wipers dragged the sand so that I couldn't even see the lines on the highway. I was sailing along the curves of the Susquehanna River, terrified.

I couldn't believe it. I wasn't saved and protected after all. I was abandoned.

I began screaming from so deep inside me I'd never felt that place before, whatever, or wherever, it was. I was suddenly in a blowout with God. I had never heard my own voice sound like that, so twisted, vicious, and cold. "What do you want from me? I've done everything I'm supposed to do! *Everything*! What more do you want to take from me? Huh? What? *What*? Who do you think you are? You're not so great. I hate you. Hate! You! God!"

Everything went blank. My car went silent. My hands buzzed on the steering wheel from the fading vibrations of my voice. With all that rage detonated, my body became hollowed out. I felt high.

I could see just enough to read a sign to Eddie's Repair. I took the next exit and found the shop. The inside of the cinder block shop was identical to my soon-to-be-ex-husband's business: the tire machine's rubber odor, a yellowed newspaper article about the shop's grand opening, a classic rock radio station blasting *Journey*. Eddie was a kind gentleman who informed me that my windshield wiper fluid was freezing. I wasn't really listening, transfixed by the tattoo on the brooding boy who fixed my car. Covering his long neck, his light brown skin read *BELOVED AND BLESSED*.

"You should be all set now, ma'am," Eddie assured me, "Deedee took care of it for you."

"Thank you," I whispered hoarsely, my blown-out voice barely there. I wrote the check, dumbfounded by Deedee. Who were these man-children with such faith? I set out on the highway.

I flew along for a few miles, then once again the fluid would not shoot out, only made a whining noise when I banged on the knob. I had gotten all my anger out, now I had come to a place of acceptance. The sun was setting on 17 West. Only a few pairs of headlights dotted

the road. Every ten minutes I'd carefully check the rear view mirror to
make sure no cars were behind me, and I'd brake to the shoulder and
take care of the sand and salt. Throwing it into park, I dashed to the
back seat to grab the heavy bottle, twisted off the child safety cap, and
doused the windshield with fluid. Then, before headlights appeared
around the bend, I gassed it back on the highway until my windshield
grew gritty again.

The fifth time, the whirling red lights of a cruiser appeared. I waited
in the highway cinders as a woman cop approached in my rear view
mirror. Before she could ask me for my license and registration, I
started frantically explaining my ridiculous situation.

"Do you need assistance?" she interrupted.

I stared at her in silence.

By the look on my face, she continued simply, "I'll follow behind
you to make sure you're okay."

Beginning my journey once again, in total darkness except for the
police lights escorting me, I decided, *Just because it's 8 degrees and
dark doesn't mean this moment isn't beautiful.* When I think back
to that drive, I'm grateful for my screams. Because since then I've
accepted that rage lives inside me. More than that, I can see the
vista clearly, that it's true God will weather my human fury, *and* I'm
beloved and blessed.

Psalm 88
A Despairing Lament

O Lord, the God of my salvation,
    I have cried out by day and in the night before You.
Let my prayer come before You;
    Incline Your ear to my cry!
For my soul has had enough troubles,
    And my life has drawn near to Sheol.

I am reckoned among those who go down to the pit;
  I have become like a man without strength,
Forsaken among the dead,
  Like the slain who lie in the grave,
  Whom You remember no more,
  And they are cut off from Your hand.
You have put me in the lowest pit,
  In dark places, in the depths.
Your wrath has rested upon me,
  And You have afflicted me with all Your waves. *Selah.*

II
You have removed my acquaintances far from me;
  You have made me an object of loathing to them;
I am shut up and cannot go out.
  My eye has wasted away because of affliction;
I have called upon You every day, O Lord;
  I have spread out my hands to You.
Will You perform wonders for the dead?
  Will the departed spirits rise and praise You? *Selah.*

III
Will Your lovingkindness be declared in the grave,
  Your faithfulness in Abaddon?
Will Your wonders be made known in the darkness?
  And Your righteousness in the land of forgetfulness?

IV
But I, O Lord, have cried out to You for help,
  And in the morning my prayer comes before You.
O Lord, why do You reject my soul?
  Why do You hide Your face from me?

I was afflicted and about to die from my youth on;
 I suffer Your terrors; I am overcome.
Your burning anger has passed over me;
 Your terrors have destroyed me.
They have surrounded me like water all day long;
 They have encompassed me altogether.
You have removed lover and friend far from me;
 My acquaintances are in darkness.
(New American Standard Bible)

In the months following my freak-out, spring neared, and as the flask filled with tears, Lola—who I also consider to be a sister—invited me to come see her when she took a job teaching metalsmithing in Italy. The most succinct way I can summarize the next passage of my spiritual journey is a couplet from Psalm 119:105: "Your word is a lamp for my feet, a light for my path."

I was led to that faith-filled country where my suffering had 100 percent prepared me to receive its fresh and holy awakenings.

I've been twice now, traveling around by train. The first time with Lola, we met up in magical Florence, then delighted in the medieval hillside town of Cortona for Holy Week. Everyone I met—students, shopkeepers, strangers—kept asking me if I had been to La Cella, a hermitage where St. Francis had lived in 1211. "You must go!" they urged me. Lola had been there with Evan, and loved it, telling me how sacred it felt, with a sign that read in English and Italian, "Stop in Silence Before God, Rediscover Who You Are."

No one had suggested that it was a stupid idea for a foreigner, a woman, to walk all by herself for an hour to a remote monastery. What about a woman with a broken inner compass? I began the journey at the edge of Cortona, near the church of Santa Margarita. What had Lola said? Take a left at the fork, then another left about a mile down, keep going. The wind gusted from the valley. I ambled around curves, to the left, to the right. Was I headed the right way? I never knew. Soon the road descended into a hamlet with a few houses, shutters flung open, an inn, a restaurant with two men outside smoking and drinking. The road spilled into another road. Had Lola instructed right or left? No matter where I went, I was perpetually getting lost, plagued by my lifelong, terrible sense of direction.

I took the left at a phone booth, found other signs, but none that read "La Cella." *But this must be the way.* I walked high up along the ridge alongside clouds so white and perfect the word that came to me was *newborn*. Not a single car passed by me. *Newborn.* The Tuscan valley and sky were mine.

Up ahead I spotted another Blessed Mother shrine, one of those crooked little buildings with rough stone walls, blotches of mortar, a wooden roof. These crooked little shrines with stone walls and wooden roofs were all over the rural roads, but who tended them? I hadn't passed any actual houses nestled in the hillsides, just the double lines of dirt tire tracks rubbed into weeds, leading to nowhere. But I never saw anyone, so who left the shelves lined with wildflower bouquets in fresh water?

I entered. Sun pierced white roses in a tin bucket. Someone had left a rock that read *Loreto.* Where Mary was born. We always thought of where Jesus was born, but about where Mary was born? Where did she begin? I would've moved into that shrine and made the roses in the glass jars my permanent address if I could have. But the sun would be setting at some point and I needed to still find La Cella.

The road dropped. I had no idea how long I had been walking. I carried no cell phone and wore no watch. At last I spied what looked like a hermitage, a building with rows of windows. And then the *La Cella* sign. I'd found it.

I descended the stone stairs down to the sign *Cella di S. Francesco. Prega en Silenzio.* I passed a few tourists and a pair of Franciscan friars in their brown robes and rope belts swinging. I couldn't help but peek to see; just like the Franciscans at my American church, they wore generic sports sandals on their feet.

I passed over another footbridge with a white waterfall cascading down a high jagged cavern. I could feel how old this place was, the rocks pressed smooth from being under rushing water for over a thousand years. Green willows blew so gently, the fronds lifting and sighing with the breezes, their tips swirling in the cool gliding water. I followed more signs, then entered the cold stone building. April shadows enveloped me. What was it like for St. Francis in the bitterness of December? How did he endure it? Voices of tourists echoed from other bridges.

Cella di S. Francesco. I entered his windowless stone room to the fragrance of huge peonies, their sweetness overflowing in a jar. His image hung, a pale ghostly face and his hand open, a halo all around him. His bed, two skinny wooden planks. His pillow, a split log. How did he rest and dream in such an austere cell? And yet I felt a presence of beauty in there.

The sun was falling. I didn't want to leave. I slowly crossed the footbridge back over the brook, photographing the water gushing over umber rock. I ascended the zigzagging stairways and gravel paths to go home. But where was *home*? Wherever it was, in Cortona or Connecticut, I had to return to it. Where did I actually dwell? And suddenly tears came.

Not like the tears I'd felt at any point in the last years or days. This gentle weeping washed me with peace as a sun shower came from the ridge. The sun shone, but rain fell on me, slanted drops dampening my hair and shoulders. I sat down on the wall of the garden to let the tears fall and just be in the rain. *I've never felt so much peace. Peace. It really does exist. And this is what it feels like. This place where St. Francis once lived and walked. Walking right on this very same path that I am on.*

Both my tears and the sun shower ended softly, simultaneously. The sun warmed my face. Would there be a rainbow? I didn't want to leave. I never wanted to leave anything I loved. I turned to take one last photograph of his cell, his door a black rectangle in a wall of gray mortar and tan stone. A bell outside his cell hung silent.

The peace stayed inside me the entire journey back. Kilometer after kilometer. I pressed my right hand between my breasts. I could breathe deeply anew. I was certain I was sending my body life messages, like Bernie Siegel encouraged me to. Was I fulfilling my promise to Dr. Vignati from that morning he told me I had no more cancer in my body, and I said, "How can I ever thank you?" And he said, "Live a good life." *Was* I living a good life? I had scars, but all the crusty specks of my blood had blown off me. I could feel it there on those mountain ridges.

I pulled the elastic out of my bun and my hair uncoiled and blew all around my face. The red circle of the sun sank through the silhouettes of the branches into the valley.

My heart began to beat wildly. I was alone. I felt it come up within me. No one could see me, or hear me, and even if they did, so what, they would just chalk it up to me being a crazy American. I shouted, "Thank you!"

It felt so good. I was shouting to God. "Thank you! Thank you!" Then, "Grazia! Gra—zeeee—ah!"

It was delicious.

By the time I reached the edge of Cortona, cypress trees rose like black flames guarding the ancient Etruscan walls. The scent of bread wafted as dogs barked and the air cooled. I stopped to check if my

photos came out. I flicked through the images. *Prega in silenzio.*
Green willows dragging their tips. And then, right in the center of
Francis' opened door, my camera captured a tiny light, a flame. Had
there been a candle I had not noticed, right where he had once lay
down his head? He was still there glowing in the dark.

Psalm 98
The Coming of God
A psalm.

I

Sing a new song to the Lord,
for he has done marvelous deeds.
His right hand and holy arm
have won the victory.
The Lord has made his victory known;
has revealed his triumph in the sight of the nations,
He has remembered his mercy and faithfulness
toward the house of Israel.
All the ends of the earth have seen
the victory of our God.

II

Shout with joy to the Lord, all the earth;
break into song; sing praise.
Sing praise to the Lord with the lyre,
with the lyre and melodious song.
With trumpets and the sound of the horn
shout with joy to the King, the Lord.

III

Let the sea and what fills it resound
the world and those who dwell there.

Let the rivers clap their hands,
 the mountains shout with them for joy,
Before the LORD who comes,
 who comes to govern the earth,
To govern the world with justice
 and the peoples with fairness.

Ruby

Sometimes, emptied of faith, a spiritual numbness overcomes me. The disconnection feels awful, but I understand it's a part of the seeking process, to not want to try anymore, to think maybe I've been a stupid Pollyanna after all, maybe the atheists are right, wanting to give up on this possibility of God, when hope seems not just hidden, but permanently eclipsed. This happened last September; my cynicism and doubt covered me. So in spite of the boulder-like coldness in my soul, I took concrete action and forced myself to drive over the mountain and attend 10:00 Mass. Because, quite frankly, I cannot bear to live in this world without God. I don't know how anyone does that. On the way into St. Patrick-St. Anthony, I asked that God just show me one sign. One thing to hang on to.

I found my usual place, the same pew by one of the pillars. I opened my missalette to the readings of that Sunday. I most frequently attend five o'clock Mass when the sun comes through the stories told in the stained glass windows on the church on the western side. That morning, the eastern angle of the sun pierced the stained glass and a pink circle of light landed upon my open pages. When I looked up to see the source, a ruby ball was so bright it hurt, and I actually had the thought, *It might be dangerous to my retinas to look right at the hotspot of the sun in Jesus' robe.*

When I had entered that church for the very first time, I was instantly transformed by the magic. Not a single window was clear. Every single arched shape told a familiar story: boats and stormy waves, a woman at a well, lambs. I felt as if I was in a cathedral-sized stained glass shell. There's nothing like that ruby-red.

It fluttered, that day, when it landed, pink. A rose, a peony, a flicker.

I believe in asking. And if all I can do is ask for one thing, I do that. If I can receive it, it ripples out and the grace widens. In that autumnal light, I noticed the brown boy sitting next to me. He had three cruci-fixes on his arm, and the most incredible eyelashes. They were long and feathery, just absolutely bird-like. I tried not to stare, but their shape was exquisite. When the collection basket was headed our way, he pulled out his wallet. Out of the corner of my eye I watched him press it open. It was empty. He had no money to give. He leaned forward and slid the wallet back into his pocket.

I wanted to cry. Not because he had no money. But because I felt I was in the same boat with this stranger next to me when I remembered my favorite Christmas song, "In the Bleak Midwinter" with lyrics by the poet Christina Rosetti.

"What can I give Him,
Poor as I am? —
If I were a Shepherd
I would bring a lamb;
If I were a Wise Man
I would do my part, —
Yet what I can I give Him, —
Give my heart."

Within

The radiance of the full moon has lasted two nights and enters my room in a soft, foggy light as I hear geese flying overhead. If I had to pick my most cherished song, and two lines of that song, I would choose "My Favorite Things" from *The Sound of Music*, with me all the way back to when I wore jumpers and saddles shoes, my braids tied with yarn. *Wild geese that fly with the moon on their wings.* I have never actually seen this happen. Will this dawn be the one, after all this time, a lifetime? I rush to the window. Through the pines, will the geese pass in front of the moon, and however briefly, carry trapezoids of light on their wings?

No, their honking disappears into the wetlands. I decide to go for a dawn walk, and as I head toward Stub Pond, I have that familiar feeling of being so glad to still be alive. The wheels of the earth spin around the sun, and now I have a limited number of springs left. We all do. Each spring becomes more priceless because of our dwindling.

As I enter the trail behind my house, it occurs to me that poetry is what happens *inside* you. The wild geese with the moon on their wings *have* flown inside me. Poetry is internal, and so is prayer. It's on the pages, walking around on the ground, but then the words lift into the light. Into you. That's where they fly.

And what I am to make of the psalms seeking me, that as I am about to close my notebook I look down and read something I have never seen before: "You shall be covered with silver as the wings of a dove, her feathers bright as gold" (Ps 68:14).

Pennies from Heaven

Finding a penny is such an ordinary thing. Just a near-worthless coin fallen in a parking lot or in cinders on the edge of a road. I absolutely love finding a penny. I keep them in a woven dish my daughter made in middle school, and when it overflows, I donate them all to the American Cancer Society, even if it's only eighty-six cents.

This began when I had the blessing of attending—or should I say the "lamps under my feet led me" to—a monthly support group with the great healer Bernie Siegel. A nebbishy Jewish pediatric surgeon from Yale who changed the face of cancer care in the 1980s with his breakout book *Love, Medicine, and Miracles*, his work has impacted the entire landscape of modern medicine ever since. His international, bestselling books—with titles like *A Book of Miracles* and *365 Prescriptions for the Soul*—are uplifting and useful to anyone, not just individuals and families traveling the unfamiliar road of serious illnesses.

We'd sit in a circle of metal folding chairs at his son's New Age bookstore, Wisdom of the Ages. Bernie's ratty, matted rescue dogs snored and panted in the center. Our group was comprised of vulnerable people in various phases of disease. Bernie holds the belief that all people long to be healed. Not cured. *Healed.* "Death is not a failure," he frequently said. "It's going to happen to all of us. But instead of being afraid of death, do something else. Send yourself *life* messages." I remember a man who was terminal; we all loved his kind smile. He had recently purchased his dream car, a vintage canary-yellow convertible Corvette, and would tell us how he traveled thirty miles (one way) each morning to go get his favorite smoothie. Bernie always praised his attitude, how the man prioritized joy and sent his body life messages.

Bernie believes in finding signs of God everywhere, including the "In God We Trust" messages imprinted on random pennies waiting for us on the ground. Bernie is a delightful storyteller, and if I recall this correctly, he tells a story of running a marathon and spying a penny many miles into his route, bending to pick it up, and hearing a spectator on the sidelines witness this and gasp, "Wow, that guy must be really poor."

A line from the psalms can glint like this.

I've flipped forward and backward through the pages. Read them right to left, from Psalm 39, turned the pages up to Psalm 116. It's just the way it is, being with them. And as I near my yearly cancer test, I tell my friend Alex how vulnerable I know I will feel in my hospital Johnny, the intimacy of being on the G.I. floor near others in their beds and just curtains between us, the chance that a stranger might see you undressing by mistake, the doctors and nurses in their New Balance sneakers, and the wait to see if Dr. Vignati found anything, and the dehydration and the anesthesia, and Alex offers, "Well, I am really glad Madeline is taking you to the test, how wonderful," and I agree. I am very grateful my children take me, and as the day of the test draws near, I am sitting on my deck with my Bible open to the Psalms and I find this glinting:

· 98 ·

The LORD sustains him on his sickbed;
>   you turn down his bedding whenever he is ill. (Ps 41:3)

I have never read those lines before, and there they are, a perfect penny found, *In God We Trust.*

Candles

On the cusp of spring, though I still need a down jacket, I sit in the wide open field and let night fall all around me. Last night the geese were through flying, walking around. I love how their wide rubbery feet lift and press on the earth, almost touching, yet are perfectly designed to not overlap as they step. They went from hushed quiet honks to silent, then simply disappeared in the dark. Like an animal myself, I turned 360 degrees to make sure no predators were coming toward me: no strangers entering the park in cars across the gravel.

Back in my neighborhood later, I kept walking. Because of the lock-down, everyone was home. I'd never seen this before, but in every single dwelling, on every street, there was rectangular light coming from within. I don't know most of my neighbors by name, but I've come to know them by their candles. There were no cars in the middle of the road, so I felt like I was on the highway, walking the double yellow line in the center. I chatted on my phone with Annie and we laughed about her son Joe's online learning adventures; even in uncertainty there is the possibility of our bodies being filled with joy.

Am I coming closer to understanding the psalms? Something is happening to me. I'm not sure what it is. Or rather, I do know. I feel a clarity, a certainty, a newfound presence right here. That God is in each of us. It's Psalm 139, becoming a part of me. I'm falling in love with the idea that we each have the light within; we're all flickering like the hundred little houses in my neighborhood, all illuminated with front doors greeting one another with the Sanskrit word *namaste*: "The light within me bows to the light within you."

Flower Power Angel

When I can't drive over the mountain into Hartford to attend my church, I go to my "backup" church across from the abandoned axe factory and man-made waterfalls along the river. With few windows and low ceilings, when the 10:00 a.m. Mass is packed, I get a bit claustrophobic. I sit in the pews on the left side near a forgotten angel I have befriended and have christened The Flower Power Angel.

The first time I noticed her, it was a welcome relief to find her there, right beside me, as I dealt with my anxiety of being too hemmed in. I realized she must've been placed there just to fill in a bare spot, and the words that came to me from *Dirty Dancing* made me laugh: "No one puts Baby in the corner." But someone *did* put Baby in the corner. This two-foot-high concrete angel with the pleasing slope of wings has been tucked alongside a wall where she can't readily be seen. She has Flower Power petals cascading down her robe that fall in a decidedly '60's motif. I almost expect some peace signs. Her posture is one of pure hope, her back arched and her expectant face uplifted.

During Mass I daydream of carrying her in my arms, walking away with The Flower Power Angel in broad daylight, just taking her, wondering if I would get busted for it, how heavy she would be, and could I lift her all by myself? Should I ask Father Collins, the one parish priest? He has a lot on his shoulders, and perhaps he'd just let me bring "Baby" home to my backyard where, like a rescue, she could be properly cherished and cared for.

Clearly, I wander far off in my thoughts during Mass. But there is one thing they do at my "backup" church that breaks through all my spacing out and misgivings about attending the church that is closer simply out of need: When the priest says, "Let your spirit come down upon these gifts to make them holy" the deacon rings Sanctus bells, and he rings them hard. The bells invite the Holy Spirit. It signals a beginning. It's such a beautiful thing. This deacon shakes them vigorously, so no matter my deep preoccupations, I'm suddenly called out of them. The fog in my mind evaporates immediately. Without even thinking about it, my eyes turn toward the altar.

The priest lifts up the host, and the bells ring, and then, when Christ is in the Eucharist, after the host and chalice are raised, the bells are rung again. Three long, bright brass shakes to confirm: He's here! These satin brass bells make the purest sound. And that deacon ensures they get stuck in your head. He lets them *go*. And I admire his vigor. It's as if he's working hard to embody the words of the psalms. "Praise him with the sounding cymbals, praise him with loud clashing cymbals / Let everything that has breath give praise to the Lord! Hallelujah!" (Ps 150:4–6).

I love how the Sanctus bells wake me from my daydreams, redirect me to what is right before me, both visible and invisible.

There's so much about the Catholic faith that I don't know (I try to think of this as a good thing, that there'll always be more layers, as opposed to feeling ill-equipped and excluded). So I researched the bells. And they're tied to the psalms. To make that joyful noise everyone talks about in the opening of Psalm 100. I learned that this ritual has been practiced for centuries, evolving from the Jewish tradition described in Exodus 40, of how to sew a sacred garment in 1440 B.C. They sought to *wear* the joyful noise, incorporating it into their fashion, which, honestly, I think would be fashionable and glamorous even today. "At the hem of the robe pomegranates were made of violet, purple, and scarlet yarn, and of fine linen twined; bells of pure gold were also made and put between the pomegranates all around the hem of the robe: a bell, a pomegranate, a bell, a pomegranate" (40:24-26). What a perfect pattern.

But I still wonder why they put The Flower Power Angel in the corner.

Streamers

It's the last day of May, and I've come to the Holy Family Monastery because my friend Lynn shared that they have an outdoor Stations of the Cross here. I'm desperate. All the churches are closed; mine rings its bells every night at 10:00 p.m. for those who have perished with the coronavirus, now 100,000 dead. The headlines are crushing; a white policeman murdered a black man this week as he was gasping for breath and crying out *Mama*. The cities in my country explode in outrage and grief. I've spent the last three months very alone in the quarantine, but I hunger for the solitude of sinking into a sacred place alone.

Whoever's designed this retreat spot has done it with thoughtfulness and maintains it with care. I'm grateful for the efforts. I can't hold the agony of that *Mama!* alone. I have no specific plan for this morning except to pray, pray slowly. An alabaster statue of Our Lady is glowing against the umber trunks of the edge of the forest. She's set high within a faux rock wall, fuchsia orchids at her feet. I will save her for last, like saving the thick top of buttercream frosting on a piece of holiday cake.

The Stations of the Cross are set along a well-worn dirt path that curves in the woods. Each station is engraved on a pewter plaque and hung within a wooden triangle on a pole to make a little roof. There are no words, just images sketched of him walking toward his murder. I can identify *Jesus Meets His Mother*. I challenge myself to name them all, though it's a bit hard to tell if Jesus has fallen. I follow a sign that reads "Labyrinth," and it takes a few long minutes of traversing in the woods to find it. It has the most breathtaking center, another faux rock tower with a deliberate huge hole in the center which encourages being at peace with emptiness, very Zen. The monastery houses an organization called the Copper Beech Institute, where they study mindfulness, yoga, and Zen teachings. It makes my heart open to wander trails that support the Christian beliefs that are mine, and the Eastern philosophies I also alight on. Merton would love it here, and I follow his example. If separate faiths can overlap, harmonize, it stirs hope.

I head back through the dappled paths to the stone benches near the parking lot. I settle in with my notebook and look up at the sturdy flagpole, thirty feet in the air with a brass knob on the top. It blows with long powder-blue and white streamers, a pair clipped to each side, north, south, east, west, made of weather-resistant material. The scantest wind lifts them. They twist and flutter. Somehow, they never get tangled, producing such a gentle sound that the bumble bee that rises is discordant in comparison. Clouds pass for a long while. The streamers move together in the sky, airborne, flying this way and that on the Peace Pole. There's no country's flag on the pole. Just streamers. Is this what people think of when they think of heaven?

Thy will be done on earth as it is in heaven.

I wonder if it could happen—could we have more heaven here on earth?

I suddenly feel a bit sick recalling that this exact spot, this past February, was vandalized. I remember the emails I received, the plea for money to help restore this sacred place. Vandals spray-painted evil messages I don't want to record here. In this tiny courtyard, some of the bricks are inlaid images of doves with feathery wings. In the opening near the benches, a carved plaque reads, "Let Us Carry the Peace of Christ into the World," and an image of human hands holds a dove, ready to be released into the sky. And near these hands, a heart has the words *Jesu Xpi Passio*. Passion of Jesus Christ. I know the vandals were not caught; they are somewhere out there, but anyone who defaces the sacred is never actually "free." How horrible it must be, to be someone who deliberately drives to a spiritual refuge to spray filth.

I can't see any of the pigments from the winter graffiti anymore. But the blight here on earth is not washed clean. It's only deepened. My heart is heavy as I pad across the soft lawn to the statue of Mary. A maple leaf has blown under an alabaster arm and clings to the folds within her sleeve. I collapse on the kneeler before her. People have expressed frustration in times of violence, the school shootings in particular, that as a country our "thoughts and prayers" aren't enough to make the changes we need to keep us all safe. Of course they aren't. But that doesn't mean I will stop praying. I believe in it. I pray. I pray that when George Floyd was crying out "Mama," and his own dead mother in heaven could not save him, that he felt Mary's embrace as she wept with him in her arms. I pray he knew she was holding him there.

Psalm 13
Prayer for Help
For the leader. A psalm of David.

I
How long, LORD? Will you utterly forget me?
How long will you hide your face from me?

How long must I carry sorrow in my soul,
    grief in my heart day after day?
    How long will my enemy triumph over me?

II
Look upon me, answer me, LORD, my God!
Give light to my eyes lest I sleep in death,
Lest my enemy say, "I have prevailed,"
lest my foes rejoice at my downfall.

Anne's Dwelling

"I've always longed to live in a place like this."

I find this beautiful sentence on page seven of my notes from my conversation with Anne, and I circle it in black ink and add stars. She had contacted me when I asked my prayer group if anyone had a special connection to the psalms, and if so would they let me interview them. I love the simplicity of her statement, and though she was specifically talking about having to suddenly find a new home recently on a small, fixed income, I think it's true that the place she's longed for and now lives is also *within*, filled with inner peace and gratitude after a lifetime of carrying a heartbreaking early wound.

We began our Zoom session, and as she appeared on my screen, I was struck by the palette of her Kelly green sweater, a lush green plant behind her, and a wash of sage on her wall. She looked lovely and smiled a warm smile as she began telling me how the psalms came to her. I was unprepared for her to begin enthusiastically sharing about the one translation that I personally had an aversion to because I think all the pigment is washed off the language in order to make it accessible. I'm not invested in the controversy among Christians about whether or not this colloquial version even counts as a "real Bible"; I just feel the translator, Eugene Peterson, rendered the tone too casual. Still, it's estimated this version has sold over twenty million copies since sections of it began being published in 1993. Clearly, readers embrace it.

"The couple that chairs the Social Justice committee at St. Patrick's open with prayer, and they use an updated version of the Bible called *The Message*. And that started me reading different parts of the Bible and I just happened to be flipping through and I thought, *Wow*. It really—the updated version—could be my life today. I enjoy reading it. That's what grabbed me about the psalms. Reading them in today's language, I was like, I get lost in the wording of the older version. That's when I get bored. So then I started noticing at church if a song said it was a psalm, I would write it down and look it up when I got home. And I was always amazed at how this related to my life today. Father Francis is really into the psalms. When he says morning Mass he always handed out a copy of a psalm that was always perfect for what I needed. With all that's been happening with COVID, I've been looking for a source of comfort. Where will I find my comfort from my fears? What I'm in love with now is Psalm 91. I've got it here. I'm just so grateful that I've been led here. I found all the other translations so boring when I was a kid at St. Mary's High School."

I said, "I'd love to hear the one from *The Message*."

She began to read:

You who sit down in the High God's presence,
spend the night in Shaddai's shadow,
Say this: "God, you're my refuge.
I trust in you and I'm safe!"

Her face took on a softness. "Right there," she wondered, "That's enough to get me through the night."

I nodded and kept my critique to myself. I know a lot about trying to get through the night. And if this version is helping her do that, I am all for it.

She continued.

That's right—he rescues you from hidden traps,
shields you from deadly hazards.
His huge outstretched arms protect you—
under them you're perfectly safe;
his arms fend off all harm.
Fear nothing—not wild wolves in the night,
not flying arrows in the day,
Not disease that prowls through the darkness,
not disaster that erupts at high noon.
Even though others succumb all around,
drop like flies right and left,
no harm will even graze you.
You'll stand untouched, watch it all from a distance,
watch the wicked turn into corpses.
Yes, because God's your refuge,
the High God your very own home,
Evil can't get close to you,
harm can't get through the door.
He ordered his angels
to guard you wherever you go.
If you stumble, they'll catch you;
their job is to keep you from falling.
You'll walk unharmed among lions and snakes,
and kick young lions and serpents from the path.
"If you'll hold on to me for dear life," says God,
"I'll get you out of any trouble.
I'll give you the best of care

if you'll only get to know and trust me.
Call me and I'll answer, be at your side in bad times;
I'll rescue you, then throw you a party.
I'll give you a long life,
give you a long drink of salvation!"

She closed the book. "This psalm is one of my favorites when I am really getting worried."

I could hear the connection to the poem in the waver of her voice. Though I knew *The Message* would never work for me, it didn't matter. Talking with Anne, something clicked inside me. In graduate school in my twenties, I'd spent three months doing nothing but reading Shakespeare's ten tragedies, reading the text while listening along for hours and hours to records of each play being performed by the British Broadcasting Company. At first, I felt beyond inept. Shakespeare made me feel stupid. But I had to press on, and eventually I began to break the code, burrowing into the language by riding inside and feeling it, and I grew to love it, though I cannot claim to have fully understood it all. Both Shakespeare and the early English translation of the psalms are from the time of King James. Even now, the King James Version of the Bible is one of the top selling versions. The King James Bible and Shakespeare have flown in tandem for centuries. Because of my background, I can see how the wings of Juliet's "this bud of love by summer's ripening breath" touch "the flood has raised its pounding waves. / More powerful than the roar of many waters, more powerful than the breakers of the sea" (Ps 93:3-4).

English doesn't have the florid touches of a Romance language like Spanish or Italian, but Shakespeare and the psalms elevate it to a higher level of musical wonder. But it can take a lot of work, and there are times it frustrates me as well.

If the psalms are finding you somehow, what does it matter what translation is alighting? I told her my belief about how the psalms seek us.

She nodded. "They find you when you most need it. When I'm not even looking, here comes a psalm that takes it all away from me. I wanted to tell a story about this exact thing! I'm living in Newington now. But I was living in Cheshire, in a tiny little place I loved. One day last October, the lady who owned it came to me and said, 'I'm really sorry, Anne, but I can't navigate the stairs in my house anymore so I need to move in here.' So, all of a sudden, I was in need of a home. It was so overwhelming to me. I thought, where am I ever going to go, on my budget, that's going to feel safe to me, and where I can feel my grandkids will be welcome to come and play.

"So someone gave me a God box. I wrote down everything I needed. Very basic, specifically a place for grandkids to play. Any apartment I looked at in my budget was awful. Awful. A week later I ran into a friend at Vespers. And she had just moved into a new place herself. And she said, 'Anne, it's beyond my wildest expectations.' And that just touched my heart.

"I said to her, 'I hope I'm saying that to you,' and in a short time, I was. You know how half of your heart feels confident you will, and the other half of your heart is terrified? I put my own ad in the paper. A week later I get a call from this guy who tells me he has an apartment in Newington, which is where both my grown daughters now live, and my grandkids. So I come to see it, and the woman living here, to turn the light on, has a tiny miraculous medal of Mother Mary. I instantly loved this place. I moved in in November. I love it more every day I am here. I can walk to both of my daughters.

"It's just so miraculous. Having seen that medal—this is definitely an answer to prayer. I have no doubt. Here I am smack dab in the

middle of both my girls. It's just so uncanny the way it all happened."
She broke into a huge smile. "This used to be a convent! Nuns used
to live here! There are only four apartments. Totally quiet. The grandkids love it here. I got all that I was looking for, and more. What I
wanted to tell you was that I then came the first line of a psalm—" She
turned the pages to find it. "Psalm 84. 'What a beautiful home.' I've
always longed to live in a place like this."

We began to laugh together. I felt giddy, absorbing her gratitude. I
asked, "So a path you never would have chosen brought you closer to
having a better life?"

"Right. Now, here I am, and I love it. The rooms are larger. I have
huge windows. And I can see the most beautiful sunsets. Which I
didn't have before. The whole thing has just been—someone has
taken care of it." Anne suddenly revealed her pain. "My mom died
when I was twenty. Two weeks before—very, very suddenly—two
weeks before I graduated from college. She had a cerebral aneurysm.
She was fine one day. Two days later she was no longer here. It was
horrible. Horrible, horrible. But things have happened that make me
say, she's right on my shoulder. She's never left me. I do think she's
had a hand in my daughters and me being in this little conclave now,
without any of us planning it. My mother was a sweet, gentle soul. I
was left with a raging alcoholic family. I was expected to handle it. No
one even hugged me at the time. But they did give me alcohol and
valium. It was a nightmare. A nightmare. She's been gone fifty years.

"But here I am living a life I would not trade with anybody.

"For decades, it was too painful for me to talk about my mother
with my daughters. But then, about eight years ago, when she was in
college, my daughter Mary wanted to know. She's always had such an
affinity for my mother, even though of course they never met. Mary
uses my mother's old cookbook, she took up Irish fiddling, became

an Irish fiddler. My mom was shipped over here from Ireland when she was four. Mary went on the Ellis Island website, and found a photo of the exact boat my mother came to America on! She found the passenger manifest with my mother's name, Margaret Flynn, and the certificate she received from going through Ellis Island. Had it all put into this huge frame. It still brings tears to my eyes. It touched my heart so deeply, because Mary and I have had, at times, a rocky road, even though now she is my best friend. At the time, we were still going through a lot of healing."

She paused. The look on Anne's face was one of maternal tenderness, that her daughter Mary brought back pieces of her long-lost mother, Margaret, and in turn, her mother brought Anne closer to both of her daughters. This is the place Anne has always longed to live.

I think of one version of Psalm 84. "How lovely is your dwelling place."

What a beautiful home.

"Every Lament Is a Love Song"

I found this quote by the writer Nicholas Wolterstork, and I embrace it fully.

Jesus lamented. He cried out the opening words of Psalm 22 as he was dying: "My God, my God, why have you abandoned me?" When you examine these words, it's clear this could only be articulated within an expectation of—and belief—in love. "My God, *my* God." Not just "God," but the God that is "mine." A love song sung from the most desperate place: death.

There's something so achingly pure about acknowledging all the times we have carried our crosses. Not self-pity, not wallowing. No, this is love for ourselves, and for the truth of how hard it's been some-times. Can we ever count how many hours of our lives we've spent silencing our song of wanting to cry out, *Why am I not being filled up with the love I so long for?*

How many times have you, or someone you know, pressed down the overwhelming grief inside them, judging their own lament? Betraying the truth of their own sorrow, their need to cry? It happens so often—but what if we think of these expressions as love songs? I think we'd accept, even welcome, their expression. Jesus quoted the psalms, and I've been moved by the assertion that Jesus *sang* the psalms as he grew up. A part of daily Jewish life, people knew them by heart. I let my imagination wander. What did Jesus sound like when he sang? You know his voice was beautiful. But not at that end. Not at that hour of torment. It was undoubtedly a gruesome and gut-wrenching sound. The lesson for us is this, I think—if Jesus turned to the psalms in his deepest hour of pain, why wouldn't we?

Fall on Your Knees

Today is the first day of summer. My annual cancer test is tomorrow. I need to "up the ante" here at home with my connection to God. I put a fresh tealight in my Our Lady of Guadalupe candle. I lie down for a few moments to just let her comfort me, and stare at the flicker and glow. How have I never noticed how the bunches of blossoming roses curve up on either side of her? I never looked closely before, and I've had this glass holder for eight years. I listen to my favorite gospel song, Tamela Mann's "Take Me to the King," while I sip my morning espresso outside and wait to see if the fresh sugar water I put in the red plastic hummingbird feeder on the shed will call to the pair of hummingbirds. They've returned for so many summers now, flying hundreds of miles—will they find their way back?

Later, upstairs, I know I'll get more relief from my anxiety if I get on my knees. I make my bed extra-neat to avoid it for a bit longer—these flashes of pride, this inner critic invading me, saying, *Why are you such a foolish sap? Falling on your knees makes no difference; it's just childish nonsense.* I take more time than usual to fold the flat sheet back over the down comforter in a perfect parallel line. Then I lean on the mattress with my hands wide open, lower to my elbows, and let myself kneel. I put my hands into prayer position and I whisper, "Stay with me."

But these words don't feel right. I rethink it, like deleting a line when I write. In the last months, this has shifted. My relationship with God has become new. I say, "Wait. No. I know you are always with me. Help *me* stay with *you*."

Despite it being the solstice, the longest day of the year, the Christmas carol "O Holy Night" comes to me. "Fall on your knees, oh hear the angel's voices." In my life, I've had my share of both depression during the relentless "holidays" and also tender, unexpected epiphanies. Now, as I stand up in my bedroom, feeling that connection I sought, I think of the words to the next stanza of the song. "And he appeared, and the soul felt its worth."

I get it now. My newfound belief that Jesus came to find me—that it only makes sense that I too am a sheep he climbed a mountain to find—has touched this place of worth at last. It's just like the shepherd Doug described, "He knows where everyone is." He knows where I am. I feel myself in the secure circle of Psalm 23, an uninterrupted, uncluttered connection to Christ. A direct, sweet dyad. An enclosure.

At long last this psalm, this carol, is true for me. He appeared. I feel my soul's worth. I am so grateful for where the psalms have led me. I don't need to try to separate out seasons into compartments. On the first day of summer, thrumming with the magic of Christmas morning, after a long, long eve, I hear that familiar sound of the tiny buzzing wings.

When the Violin

When
The violin
Can forgive the past
It starts singing...
When the violin can forgive
Every wound caused by
Others
The heart starts
Singing.
　—Hafiz

The psalms have become ocean waves now, washing across into the New Testament, shushing and unfurling, high tide coming in, wetting the sand, receding, then covering it. I hadn't expected the psalms to pack this much of a gravitational pull toward Jesus. I can't even call it a "renewal" because it's just, quite simply, new. For me, the understanding of beginning again, of forgiving, from Psalm 51 flows right into what Jesus says of children in Matthew 18:5. "And whoever received one child such as this in my name receives me."

Yes, I'm trying to say something about forgiving my father.

Psalm 51 and the hyssop.

"The bones you have crushed will rejoice" (51:10).

My father's nickname for me is *Bones*.

The bones you have crushed.

In the guest bedroom of my parents' house, my mother has stashed all the stacked bins of our family's ephemera. There's a photo of my father that I believe holds his true spirit, his original innocence. In it, my father is a skinny little thing, around five or six, the eyes of his child-self looking very similar to his adult-self, his lids squinting. He's posing on a Long Island beach in an old timey-one-piece bathing suit with thin black straps over his elfin shoulders, his arms draped proudly around his siblings as he stares into the camera.

He's just a little boy.

I don't have a copy of this photo. But several years ago, my mom and I were in a junk store and I came across an old photograph that called to me. I bought it and put it in a gold frame and I have it on my wall now.

I now see how it's the spiritual story of my father. *Dad as a child running free.* There's a boy in it, running fast, into the sea, for the joy of it. There's a palace-like building set back from the sand rising with a magical dome. Every beachgoer is turned toward the tide. A mother is holding up the hem of her dress; her young daughter enters an empty rowboat. A few men are enjoying the sunny afternoon, the cut of their vests in three-piece suits and the brim of their jaunty newspaper caps is of the 1930s, the decade my father was a child, years before he disappeared to Korea, became a sniper in the war.

Boys are dashing gleefully into the gunmetal-gray surf. One kicks at the spray of a breaking wave, the others bolt, tilting forward with arms angled behind thin bodies. The most prominent boy in the picture, the one I now see as my father, leans in his inky one-piece bathing suit, not diving, but with arms eagerly outstretched to enter the water.

His hands are open, ahead of the other boys, he's the winner, the first one, clearly elated to be letting go, his face in the sun, meeting the wave he fears will crash into him head on and knock him down, and it will, but it will also take him in and wash him clean.

When the Branches Catch It All

On my cell phone, I keep my "to do" list of all the things I need to keep track of to keep my life running smoothly, and I check it, add to it, or delete things dozens of times a day. I also keep affirmations to read during the busy days, as a way of "ordering my steps in thy word." I don't know where this came from, but every time I put something on the list or cross it off, I read, "Gentleness of Christ within. God seeking me instead of me seeking God." I must have read this hundreds of times, alongside that other favorite quote from John O'Donohue, "May you take the time to celebrate the quiet miracles that seek no attention." Now, combined with the psalms, it seems there are more tender things in this world. Were they always here? If so, where was I?

I've noticed that when I read the psalms in the morning now, when I hear that soft sound of the pages turning, so tissue-thin, that it's not just my finger*tips*, but even tinier—my finger*prints* can flip them.

Gentle: *as in, dove-like.*

I'm curious, how do all the words fit together? When I wake up, I begin my day by pulling back the curtains and thinking my favorite line, "This is the day the Lord has made; let us rejoice in it and be glad" (Ps 118:24). I have *this* day now. The snow fell last night when I was dreaming, just enough, airy enough, to cling to the trees on top, not fall beneath them, only land in a scallop beyond the wide arms of the branches. There's no white underneath, just the copper of the dead needles. I want a God like the softest of snowfalls when the branches can catch it all. A God as tiny as the letter "e" at the end of a word, turning "breath" to "breathe."

The Key in Assisi

The mark of motherhood is permanently on me, and I cannot imagine who I would be, spiritually, if I had not been gifted with two remarkable children, my daughter and my son. Motherhood stretches you, both stretches your body in ways you never knew it could go, and spreads open your ability to love. I began writing by titling this section "Assisi" and ended up at motherhood. Which is fitting: these are the two most spiritual places I've been.

After I went to Italy the first time with Lola and Evan, I felt called to return. I didn't know it, but my steps were being ordered. Around Christmas, I found the listing of an artists' colony in Assisi that looked perfect for me to stay at the following summer of 2016. I worked hard on my application with writing samples, sent it, and was accepted within forty-eight hours. The whole trip was so transformative, it still confounds me how smoothly the whole thing happened. I went gliding.

I flew to Florence and took the train to Assisi. One sweltering afternoon I sat in one of the holy spots, the church called Mary of the Angels. Franciscan priests from all over the world milled around speaking all languages. I watched them in their brown robes, gesturing and trying to keep their voices down, but still talking excitedly. It was clear how inspired and touched they were being near St. Francis's little chapel, a tiny church inside the church. It was moved there from elsewhere in Assisi and was one of Francis's main places to pray.

I watched them take their turns entering, thinking how wonderful it was that all these friars could come on this pilgrimage. This special trip to a sacred town, visiting all the relics. I then burst out laughing. *I was on a pilgrimage!* I was visiting everything they were. I was having the time of my life writing up in the artists' colony and walking the mountains where Francis walked. I had wept at Clare's bones in the Basilica of Santa Chiara. I'd sat for an hour in front of the Cross of San Damiano. I'd spent a whole day staring at the Giotto frescos at the Basilica di San Francesco. How did this happen? I was a pilgrim on a pilgrimage! It seemed so uncool, at first. Which is a ridiculous thing to think, but there it was. Very quickly the feeling of embarrassment passed and gave way to a pride radiating from my gut. This is who I was. I thought of that day I'd witnessed the pilgrimage of the walkers carrying crosses from Santa Fe to Chimayo. I'd become one of them. Someone willing to travel far to find.

The Porziuncola ("little chapel") glowed yellow on the outside, the walls waxy. Completely intact and protected inside the basilica, it had the feel of finding an enchanting children's playhouse within a forest, but I don't mean that in a disrespectful way. It's just the scale of it, I think. You had to wait your turn to go in, because you could only fit a few people; there were maybe three rows of pews and behind that, a few places to kneel.

Francis' *porziuncola* was the coziest, sweetest, safest home. I loved it so much. It finally came my turn to enter. How can I keep unlocking all the love within me? That tiny chapel was an overflowing heart. I entered it and turned. I felt something open. I was the key.

The Billboard

I was talking to my friend Patrick and his husband one day about changes in our lives. How you go through various stages and can only identify them when you look back.

I said, "I moved out here, to begin a new life, and for several years this was my 'new life.' But where is that line where it just becomes your life, your present life? Now this is just my life, after six years. It's not my 'new' life."

I've thought about this since we had these realizations together. Talking with people, all of us are always amazed at "where the time has gone," particularly when raising children. At a party the other night, a father of four daughters was saying how he looked out his back door at one of his daughters and said to his wife, "Oh, I didn't know Abby came back already."

His wife responded, "That's not Abby. It's Maggie."

The husband said to us, with a wistful expression around the fire pit, "Maggie's changed, and she looks older, like, overnight."

These changes. Our faces. Our children's faces. Moving from one state or city to another, from the various gradations of loss and healing, we can't expect ourselves to know where those lines are and when we cross them. My movement into worthiness did not come as a great epiphany, some sort of geyser or celestial event in the sky. All the awakenings in my life have led me here.

This last half year of reading the psalms invited something into me I didn't plan for, or aim for, or even think existed. I don't know when it happened. I do know that Psalm 23 is at the core.

My ex-student Megan has been living in Spain and we FaceTimed yesterday for hours. In all honesty, there are not many people I would speak like this to and I took advantage, trying to get clarity.

"It's so personal," I exclaimed.

"Maureen, I give you a lot of credit. It takes courage to talk about your faith. Sometimes when I tell people I'm Episcopalian, they're like, but that's *organized religion*."

We laughed, her lip-ring glinting in the sun.

I went on. "So, I went back over some of the spiritual writing I did last year for my Mary blogs. And I was blown away because I saw the theme of my unworthiness. How I was expressing that I felt so unworthy of God's love, and left out at times. It's like something inside me got filled up. I feel God with me all the time. I feel less lonely. I've struggled with loneliness my whole life, and now, I just don't feel that."

"Wow, that is amazing."

"And the thing is, I took on this project as a poet, as a woman of faith, but I wanted to just write about the psalms. I didn't want to put Jesus at the center. But now what's true is that I feel so much of him. It's like I understand that I'm the sheep. It dawned on me that even if I was the special one who was lost, he would still come find me. It just didn't make sense anymore that I would be left out. It was like I was suddenly inside the setting of Psalm 23, and he was there. And I feel so vulnerable in putting this in the world. I had no intention of writing about Jesus."

My genuine bafflement made us both laugh again.

So imagine my continued amazement when, months later, after Megan returned from Spain and we met on the Rails-to-Trails Bridge over the Farmington River in Collinsville, she showed me her tattoos of angels on her calves that represent a line from "O Holy Night."

"Yes, Maureen," she said, "they represent the line 'the soul felt its worth.'"

How lucky am I to have students who become my friends? And who tattoo themselves with Christmas carols.

+ + +

In September 2016, I went to Lola's wedding. As I drove through Georgia a billboard caught my attention: JESUS, it read in black letters, on a yellow background. Nothing else but that. No ad for a Baptist church, or a Christian nonprofit, no number to call, just JESUS. I began to think of my father's mother, May, her name a diminutive of Mary. Driving in the back of the van, the appearance of JESUS in capital letters brought it all back. I remembered May saying, over tea, "Reenie, your father loves you." I never knew why she would tell me that. I remember her saying, "Your father was different before he went to Korea. He came back different."

Her death had changed me, but I had never spoken of it. I kept it inside, another secret. She died in 1992. It was horrible. She was in the hospital, near the end. She had become unglued and it broke my heart. She understood what I was saying, but she could no longer speak. Her familiar blue eyes, exactly like my father's, were floating in opposite directions, and I knew I was losing her. I had never seen eyes move like that, one headed east and one headed west. I was grateful for those recent years I had with her, during my twenties, after I got sober; I often drove to Mount Kisco to see her alone and be her granddaughter. She'd read to me from her autobiography that she was writing on yellow legal pads. We'd drink Lipton tea and eat gingersnaps because that was the only treat she was allowed with her diabetes. We laughed really hard when she read me the racy parts about meeting her future husband, Ray O'Brien.

The year I met Tim, who would be my future husband, I brought him with me, and she loved him at first sight because with his beard he looked identical to Josh on *The Guiding Light,* her favorite actor on her favorite soap opera. When we took her out for Chinese food, she insisted on holding his arm and walking into the restaurant with him, joking that he was her younger boyfriend. To the end, she was both flirtatious and vain.

When we sat in her living room, she often steered the conversation to death.

"I'm scared to die. Reenie, do you think I'll go to heaven?" She'd turn very serious.

"Of course, Grandma, you're a good person."

"I've only been with one man in my whole life, so I think God will reward me for that."

Ray left her with five children when she was thirty-seven years old; when my father was a boy of eight.

Those afternoons with my grandmother and my fiancé were among my happiest of my life.

"If you ever lay a hand on her, you'll have to deal with me," she'd say to him, making her knobby arthritic hand into a fist and shaking it.

Tim and I married. There is a photo from my wedding with both my grandmothers in the back of their limo, deep in conversation, both wearing peplum dresses. Within a year, I had given birth to Madeline, and a few years later, Grandma May lay in that hospital room.

"I'm pregnant again," I whispered to her, two months along with my son. I brushed her hair. Her eyes widened, sky and clouds; she was disappearing.

I still regret how I tried to fix her hair. I was trying to cover my sadness by being brave. I combed her bangs up off her face and secured them with a barrette in the shape of a bow. She would have never put her hair into such a silly style.

I said, "Grandma, are you scared?"

She shook her head no, emphatically. Back and forth, NO. At that moment I felt the presence of Jesus. It wasn't something I believed existed, until her deathbed, and it wasn't anything I sought or courted. But it was undeniable. I felt him walk through her, I felt immense safety, he was taking care of her and he was *taking* her, and I felt a glow that was comforting and familiar. This orb, this warm glow, widened all around us, Grandma, Jesus, me, and Max-at-two-months within me. Then, like a rainbow, he dissipated. I burst into tears, and I knew it was time to say goodbye to her. I said, "I love you so much, Grandma." She put her lips to my cheek but was unable to pucker. She was shutting down. As I left, the nurse outside her door said, "She's a sweetie!"

My Grandma May died that night.

I inherited two things. My aunt gave me one of Grandma May's wedding bands. My grandparents had never divorced. My grandfather had been, allegedly, "as handsome as Robert Redford"; I took her Sacred Heart picture, the one of the Jesus with eyes that follow you, not in a creepy way, but sort of feminine and pretty. It's behind me right now as I write.

I know that encounter with Jesus is what some people label being "born again." This label scared me. The moments of his love went deep inside my heart, one of the most profound moments of my life, being pregnant with my child while being with my father's dying mother, and having Jesus enter. This experience was ineffable; I never spoke of it. I kept it a secret because I believed that if I tried to put it into words, it would tarnish the shine of it. I never understood it. May had been terrified of dying up until the moments she actually died and he came for her. Then, walking through the valley of death, she was no longer afraid. How had I forgotten that part?

I didn't know where all my seeking would lead. I didn't know it would take me to Sermon on the Mount. "Ask and it will be given to you, seek and you will find; knock and the door will be opened to you" (Matthew 7:7). It's like the allegorical painting by William Holman Hunt, *The Light of the World.* Jesus is knocking expectantly on the door, but there's no handle. It only opens from the inside.

It took me decades to let him in.

Psalm 23

I have a place in my life that's like the setting of Psalm 23. Haywire Farm, thirty minutes north of me, almost to Massachusetts, has a modest gray house and emerald green barn at the top of the hill. The six-acre slope of land has three large fenced paddocks. One, behind the barn, where the five horses mostly graze, another one where they practice jumping, and a third, closer to Case Street, overgrown with clover and daisies.

It's a place of refuge. Amy, the woman who created this farm, has set a goal of making this a sanctuary with an open-door policy where any person seeking the healing beauty of horses is welcome. "I think of Psalm 23 when I look over the land. I always feel watched over here."

All five horses get everything they need to thrive. Equine dentists for their enormous teeth. A farrier to scrape out and whittle down their hooves and make them sound and safe to canter and gallop upon. They get annual shots for diseases such as Eastern Equine Encephalitis and Strangles. Each horse has its own generous stall, with a window cranked open to pastoral views. In summer, the pointy ears of their fly masks rip and at night Amy sews them back up. In winter they each have their own jewel-tone blankets, dyed emerald and plum. For rain all year round, each one has its own rain sheet with the amusing brand name of Rambo. Captain is the tiny crabby leader. Rex is the gentle giant. Salt licks are tied up with ropes, placed near their windows. They're sprayed for bugs to keep them calm and cool. The hay nets both outside and in the barn are filled again and again, all day long. The stalls are mucked from morning to night, and almost always the stall matts are fluffy with fresh shavings. There's a constant squeak of the water pump being spun in the barn for the fresh water to gush and fill up all their buckets—which the plentiful barn swallows swooping in and out of the windows poop in. The work of loving them and caring for them is endless.

The horses understand that the people who come to Haywire are seeking to slow themselves down and join with them in the moment. Of course, there are so many connections between Psalm 23 and Jesus, but my favorite is "Those who are well do not need a physician, but the sick do. Go and learn the meaning of the words, 'I desire mercy'" (Matthew. 9:13). It's not perfect—no place is; there are hounds that run through, and snakes in the woodpiles. But I include myself in the number of people who go to the farm to be restored. I don't know how or why, but it melts my fears to watch the horses' changing silhouettes. Because my bones break so easily, I don't risk riding them. But I don't have to. They delight me with their hilarious side-eyes and eyerolls, the way the gorgeous thoroughbred pony Timmy says he loves me by blowing hard through his velvet muzzle and deliberately fogging up my glasses.

The transformations that occur are striking. There's the seven-year-old girl who, after a meltdown at school during a fire drill refused to go back, and only returned to school once she began riding the horses at Haywire. A fifty-five-year-old man who suffered with painful physical disabilities his whole life, including pain in both hips because one of his legs is shorter than the other, comes every week.

· 134 ·

Amy tells me how in twenty years of knowing him, she never saw him smile until he started to ride. He smiles all the time now and says he made three good decisions in his life: to get sober, to get married, and to ride at Haywire. "It's my church," he says.

The mothers come. A mother who lost her child to cerebral trauma after he shot himself. A mother whose daughter passed without being able to say goodbye: The daughter didn't allow her own mother to come see her when she was dying. The mothers of grown children in prison. These women now stand in the stalls, cooing softly and brushing the dusty flanks, and together they spent last August painting every side of the barn.

On any given Sunday, the little girls run past the wilted rhubarb in their cool cowboy boots, joyfully wanting to give Tonka and Levi carrots. You would not know these kids were labeled ADHD, depression, defiance, social anxiety, suicidality, social anxiety. There is a sixteen-year-old girl named Grace who has become a fixture at Haywire. She had once been a truant. I ask if she would tell me about her connection to the farm. But first, I read her Psalm 23.

She laughs, her head a crown of long roan braids lightly blowing and her brown eyes very wise for someone others would refer to as "a kid." She nods. "It's a safe space. And oh—you got the green pastures right on! You've got plenty of shepherds with Amy and the horses here. Even sweeping the barn is an escape. It's a piece of heaven touching the clouds. I bet in the morning you can touch them." Her description is lovely.

"So how did you end up here? How did you find this place?"

Grace's eyes grow serious. "I ran away in January. I was looking for an escape. I went away for three days. I was free. It was snowing and cold. My parents were in the streets of Hartford looking for me. I was in an abandoned apartment. I ran away Friday and woke up in an unused Airbnb with a strange lady standing over me. She asked, 'Who are you?' She prayed over me. Pleading. 'I hope she finds her way home, God please take care of her. Forgive her. Please keep Grace safe.' She told me she had awakened at 4:00 a.m., with a message inside her head: 'Check your Airbnb upstairs.' And that's how she found me.

"But I wasn't done running away. I went home and snuck out again that night to get on the bus to Hartford with my friend, a boy who was a troubled kid. His mom was absent. His dad was absent. But his parents weren't looking for him like mine were. My mom had called the police that time. They put posters out for me. I ended up in a freezing place with homeless people walking through the hallways, and holes where the doorknob was supposed to be. It was exhilarating and sad. At last, I went back home.

"My grandma is really good friends with Amy. She was like, 'You're going to Haywire.' I ended up here in February. Ever since then I haven't had the urge to run away anywhere. I have this outlet now. If I run away, I can't come here. Why would I want to run from this? Riding a horse, you become one with it. When I ride, everything turns off and I flow. You're untouched and pure, what you are meant to be.

"My anger and the turmoil inside me—if it was a dust storm, it's now the last line you try and sweep into the dust pan. Still there, but barely noticeable. I can breathe again. One night when I slept over here, I woke up and came outside, and I was like, I want to lay in the grass and be merged into the earth. To feel at peace."

"So," I ask, "What would you call it? God? Great Spirit? The Divine?"

She shakes her head in wonder. "All I know is there's something out there. And it's not asking for anything. But it wants us to be open to receiving."

We sit in a profound silence for a long time. I think of how God never asked me for anything. Just wanted to give. How I have learned to receive. Grace stands up and heads into the barn. A few moments later she comes out leading the enormous Rex, and she hops on him bareback. They look perfect together. Grace circles the outside of the paddock, and I think of all the people who love her so deeply, who searched for her when she was lost.

The logo for Haywire Farm, when you turn into the driveway at the mailbox, is made of a round oval with barbed-wire twining around. In the center, untouched by any pain, a graceful, simple-lined horse leaps wide in teal and green. All of us go to Haywire—or to church, or to the ocean, or to the psalms—to find that spirit within, to find, again, the one within us who runs free.

The Nun at San Damiano

I can still see her white robes and headdress as she popped in and out of the windows at San Damiano. This sacred site is where St. Francis's soul-sister, St. Clare, lived and died in Assisi in the 1200s. The long, slow walk up to the monastery through the olive groves set a tone of inner reflection. The solstice view stretched for miles as we brushed against the magenta hibiscus blossoms backlit in terracotta pots. We could feel the deepening peace of the enclave of Clare.

As in all of the holy sites, the signs, written in many languages, remind visitors that taking photographs is simply forbidden. And yet, that day, a nun in a starched cream-colored habit, a novice perhaps, a future Bride of Christ in the Umbrian light, a visitor like the rest of us, was exuberantly running around with her iPad photographing everything. Young and quick and agile, she was recording the chipped wings of the angel frescos, the worn, rough steps leading to the room where Clare died, the silhouette of the tower bell. I could feel both myself and the others in the crowd grow annoyed. But she was oblivious, joyfully capturing it all in spite of the fact that she was trampling, or even, trespassing. The cool stone rooms filled with murmurs and tongues clicking, people appalled at her behavior. She was a *nun*! At a *holy site*!

As we moved through an open corridor, breathing in the tranquility and learning the Poor Clare history, the nun suddenly poked out of an upper window like a jack-in-the-box with her iPad lifted. She took a few fast shots, then disappeared. The humor of it hit us. Laughter rippled. Not in meanness, but at the absurdity of a nun breaking the rules while the rest of us were obeying them. She was not acting right, and it wasn't fair to the rest of us, who also wanted to take photos. But she was actually quite graceful, swaying, bobbing, and dancing with such abandon around the medieval rooms, that we began to delight in her. Perhaps this is a stretch, but I would like to believe that our mutual love of Jesus led us all to a softer place, in the words of Clare: "We become what we love, and who we love shapes what we become."

We were near the end of the tour when I spied the nun ahead of me. She had put her iPad down on a bench and was headed into a darkened arch of votive candles to begin praying. And I pulled my Coolpix camera out of my purse and *I* took a picture of *her* from the back in the gorgeous afternoon light. Was I now breaking the rules in photographing her? I didn't care.

Later, I was stunned. Out of the thousands of pictures I have taken in Italy, it is by far my best shot, full of mystery. The shape of her head under the headscarf, the triangular way it drapes over her shoulders and hangs down her back, the contrast of sun and shadow in the pleats of the material, the humble little straight pin fastening the cloth to her hair lurking underneath. Facing away from any camera, turned toward God, light folds over her, making her glow from within, radiating wings.

Let Us Begin Again

There's a poster that reads, *"Let us begin again,"* St. Francis of Assisi, with a speckled bird soaring above the looping letters.

Us, not *me*. Begin again. It doesn't say "begin again while looking back at the past that still hurts and confounds us" or "begin again while worrying about the bad things that might happen in the future." I've been studying psalm-words—*Lord, refuge, mercy*—and isolating them, but now I need to put them back together. I disassembled the psalms to examine them closely, like a leaf under a microscope, finding the opening and closing of the stomata. But the true beauty of a leaf, like our human lives, exists when you watch it bud, grow, and fall with all the other leaves. Together. So I am looking out over the breathtaking view of the psalms as I hope we never forget to begin, again and again. To know, no matter what, that we are walking in love and beauty when we seek.

Then our mouths were filled with laughter;
  our tongues sang for joy...

Those who sow in tears
Will reap with cries of joy.

Those who go forth weeping,
 Carrying sacks of seed,
Will return with cries of joy,
 Carrying their bundled sheaves.
(Ps 126:2, 5-6)

Notes

1. Thomas Merton, *Bread in the Wilderness* (New York: New Directions Books, 1953) 59.
2. Merton, *Bread in the Wilderness*, 32.
3. "Richard Rohr on Merton"; https://blog.franciscanmedia.org/franciscan-spirit/richard-rohr-on-thomas-merton.
4. Merton, *Thoughts in Solitude* (New York:Farrar, Strauss, and Giroux, 1999), 79.
5. C.S. Lewis, *Reflections on the Psalms* (San Francisco: HarperOne, 2017) 51.
6. Lao Tzu, *The Tao Te Ching Book of the Way and of Righteousness*, Translation and Commentary by Charles Johnston (Vancouver, Canada: Kshetra Books, 2016).
7. Michael Wilson, "The Morgue Worker, the Body Bags and the Daffodils," *New York Times*, May 5, 2020.

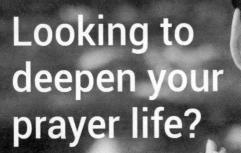